MONEY

THE CAMBRIDGE ECONOMIC HANDBOOKS

General Editors

J. M. KEYNES (Lord Keynes)	1922–1936
D. H. ROBERTSON (Sir Dennis Robertson)	1936–1946
C. W. GUILLEBAUD	1946–1956
C. W. GUILLEBAUD ⎫ MILTON FRIEDMAN ⎭	1956–

MONEY

SIR DENNIS ROBERTSON

Fellow of Trinity College, Cambridge
Emeritus Professor of Political Economy
in the University of Cambridge

DIGSWELL PLACE
JAMES NISBET & CO. LTD.
CAMBRIDGE
AT THE UNIVERSITY PRESS

First published *1922*
Revised *1924*
Reprinted *1926, 1927*
Revised and reset *1928*
Reprinted *1930, 1932, 1935*
Reprinted with new preface *1937*
Reprinted *1940, 1941, 1943, 1944, 1945,*
1946 (twice)
Revised with additional Chapters . . *1948*
Reprinted . . . *1948, 1951, 1954, 1956*
Reset *1959*
Reprinted *1961*
Reprinted *1966*

INTRODUCTION

TO THE CAMBRIDGE ECONOMIC HANDBOOKS
BY THE GENERAL EDITORS

SOON after the war of 1914–18 there seemed to be a place for a series of short introductory handbooks, 'intended to convey to the ordinary reader and to the uninitiated student some conception of the general principles of thought which economists now apply to economic problems'.

This Series was planned and edited by the late Lord Keynes under the title 'Cambridge Economic Handbooks' and he wrote for it a General Editorial Introduction of which the words quoted above formed part. In 1936 Keynes handed over the editorship of the Series to Mr. D. H. Robertson, who held it till 1946, when he was succeeded by Mr. C. W. Guillebaud.

It was symptomatic of the changes which had been taking place in the inter-war period in the development of economics, changes associated in a considerable measure with the work and influence of Keynes himself, that within a few years the text of part of the Editorial Introduction should have needed revision. In its original version the last paragraph of the Introduction ran as follows:

'Even on matters of principle there is not yet a complete unanimity of opinion amongst professional economists. Generally speaking, the writers of these volumes believe themselves to be orthodox members of the Cambridge School of Economics. At any rate, most of their ideas about the subject, and even their prejudices, are traceable to the contact they have enjoyed with the writings and lectures of the two economists who have chiefly influenced Cambridge thought for the past fifty years, Dr. Marshall and Professor Pigou.'

Keynes later amended this concluding paragraph to read:

'Even on matters of principle there is not yet a complete unanimity of opinion amongst professional students of the subject. Immediately after the war (of 1914–18) daily economic events were of such a startling character as to divert attention from theoretical complexities. But today, economic science has recovered its wind. Traditional treatments and traditional solutions are being questioned, improved and revised. In the end this activity of research should clear up controversy. But for the moment controversy and doubt are increased. The writers of this Series must apologize to the general reader and to the beginner if many parts of their subject have not yet reached to a degree of certainty and lucidity which would make them easy and straightforward reading.'

Many though by no means all the controversies which Keynes had in mind when he penned these words have since been resolved. The new ideas and new criticisms, which then seemed to threaten to overturn the old orthodoxy, have, in the outcome, been absorbed within it and have served rather to strengthen and deepen it, by adding needed modifications and changing emphasis, and by introducing an altered and on the whole more precise terminology. The undergrowth which for a time concealed that main stream of economic thought to which Keynes referred in his initial comment and to which he contributed so greatly has by now been largely cleared away so that there is again a large measure of agreement among economists of all countries on the fundamental theoretical aspects of their subject.

This agreement on economic analysis is accompanied by wide divergence of views on questions of economic policy. These reflect both different estimates of the quantitative importance of one or another of the conflicting forces involved in any prediction about the consequences of a policy measure and different value judgments about the desirability of the predicted outcome. It still remains as true today as it was when Keynes wrote that—to quote once more from his Introduction:

'The Theory of Economics does not furnish a body of settled conclusions immediately applicable to policy. It is a method rather than a doctrine, an apparatus of the mind, a technique of thinking, which helps its possessor to draw correct conclusions.'

This method, while in one sense eternally the same, is in another ever changing. It is continually being applied to new problems raised by the continual shifts in policy views. This is reflected in the wide range of topics covered by the Cambridge Economic Handbooks already published, and in the continual emergence of new topics demanding coverage. Such a series as this should accordingly itself be a living entity, growing and adapting to the changing interests of the times, rather than a fixed number of essays on a set plan.

The wide welcome given to the Series has amply justified the judgment of its founder. Apart from its circulation in the British Empire, it has been published from the start in the United States of America, and translations of the principal volumes have appeared in a number of foreign languages.

The present change to joint Anglo-American editorship is designed to increase still further the usefulness of the Series by expanding the range of potential topics, authors and readers alike. It will succeed in its aim if it enables us to bring to a wide audience on both sides of the Atlantic lucid explanations and significant applications of 'that technique of thinking' which is the hallmark of economics as a science.

C. W. GUILLEBAUD

April 1957   MILTON FRIEDMAN

PREFACE TO THE FOURTH EDITION

THANKS, as I am constantly being informed, mainly to its chapter-headings, this book, in spite of not having been revised since 1928, still finds a market. I cannot allow this state of affairs to continue; but in view of all that has happened since 1928 I should find the book quite impossible to revise. I have therefore made no change in the old text except to introduce a needed refinement into the handling of one topic (the various meanings of 'the value of money') in Chapter II, and to cut out some little bits of specially dead wood (about index-numbers of prices) in the same chapter. But I have added two new chapters (IX and X), the one mainly narrative, the other more argumentative, in order to give the reader some idea of what has been going on, in the realms both of fact and of theory, since the book was last re-written. (The two new chapters are printed *after* the little symbolic appendices, so as to make it plain that the latter are part of the old book.)

It is important therefore that the reader who, in 1947 or later years, embarks on the book should realise clearly what he is doing. In the first eight chapters he will be looking at the world of 1928 through the eyes of 1928. He must not assume that all the statements of fact made in these chapters still hold good, or even that all of those which do not will be systematically corrected for him in Chapter IX. Nor must he assume that, if I were starting afresh, I should now invite him to approach the study of Money in exactly the same way. Provided this is understood, I venture to hope that the book will still be found to possess a certain measure of interest and usefulness. Anyway, there are still the chapter-headings—and two more of them.

In Chapter X I have made use of a few sentences which

formed part of a talk broadcast in May 1947 and printed in
The Listener.

I append §§ 2 to 4 of the preface to the 1937 reprint of the
1928 edition.

*   *   *   *   *   *

§ 2.   The book is intended to be a more or less self-contained
unit: but it was also in its original form the second volume of
a series.   Its connection with its predecessor—Mr. Henderson's
Supply and Demand—is to be found in the emphasis laid on
the theory of money as a special case of the general theory of
value.   Its bearing upon the remainder of the series is to be
found in the conclusion to which the book leads up, that
Money is after all a subject of secondary importance, in the
sense that neither the most revolutionary nor the 'soundest'
monetary policy can be expected to provide a remedy for those
strains and disharmonies whose roots lie deep in the present
structure of industry, and perhaps in the very nature of man
himself.

§ 3.   This is a work of exposition and not of research.   I have
therefore availed myself freely, and (except on a few rather
special points) without detailed acknowledgment, of the ideas
and the labours of others.   I owe a great debt to the standard
writings of Marshall, Pigou, Cassel, Knapp, Irving Fisher,
Hawtrey, Taussig and Withers: and on the subject matter of
Chapter VI to the works of Gregory and Jack.   The im-
measurable debt which both the original and the 1928 editions
of this book owed to Mr. J. M. Keynes has not been diminished
by the lapse of time.   I have made use of ideas and of a few
passages contained in my *Banking Policy and the Price Level*
and in a lecture on *Theories of Banking Policy* reprinted in
Economic Essays and Addresses (both published by P. S. King
& Son).

§ 4.   When a conclusion previously reached is being used as
the basis for a fresh argument, I have often been obliged, for

the sake of brevity, to content myself with a mere page-reference, instead of helping the reader by restating the conclusion at length.   The reader who is irritated by these sign-posts is entitled to neglect them: but if he neglects them, he forfeits the right to complain that the new argument is putting too great a strain on his memory or his understanding.   No reader is under any obligation to look at the two appendices.

D. H. R.

CAMBRIDGE,
   May 1947

CONTENTS

CHAPTER I

THE MERITS AND DRAWBACKS OF MONEY

CHAPTER II

THE VALUE OF MONEY

I. WHAT IS MEANT BY THE VALUE OF MONEY

II. HOW THE VALUE OF MONEY IS DETERMINED

CHAPTER III

THE QUANTITY OF MONEY

I. THE KINDS OF MONEY

II. THE QUANTITY OF BANK MONEY

III. THE QUANTITY OF COMMON MONEY

CHAPTER IV

THE GOLD STANDARD

CHAPTER V

MONEY AND SAVING

CHAPTER VI

MONEY IN THE GREAT MUDDLE

I. MONETARY COLLAPSE

II. MONETARY RESTORATION

CHAPTER VII

THE QUESTION OF THE STANDARD

CHAPTER VIII

THE QUESTION OF THE CYCLE

CHAPTER IX

MONEY IN THE SECOND GREAT MUDDLE

CHAPTER X
PROBLEMS OF WORDS, THOUGHT AND ACTION

2

CHAPTER I

THE MERITS AND DRAWBACKS OF MONEY

'Crabs and all sorts of things,' said the Sheep: 'plenty of choice, only make up your mind. Now what *do* you want to buy?'

Through the Looking-glass

§ **1. Introductory.** Money is not such a vital subject as is often supposed; nevertheless, it is an interesting and important branch of the study of economics. It is necessary for the economic student to try from the start to pierce the monetary veil in which most business transactions are shrouded, and to see what is happening in terms of real goods and services; indeed so far as possible he must try to penetrate further, and to see what is happening in terms of real sacrifices and satisfactions. But having done this he must return and examine the effects exercised upon the creation and distribution of real economic welfare by the twin facts that we do use the mechanism of money, and that we have learnt so imperfectly to control it.

The necessity for such an enquiry became especially obvious in the years immediately after the war, when the monetary systems of the world were thoroughly out of order. For a monetary system is like a liver: it does not take up very much of our thoughts when it goes right, but it attracts a deal of attention when it goes wrong. In those days almost everybody became acutely aware of the violent changes which were taking place in the purchasing power of money over the things which he wished to buy; and most people became also, though less vividly, aware of the violent changes which were taking place in the purchasing power of the money of their own countries over the money of other countries. We have now entered

1

calmer waters once more. The monetary problems of to-day are less spectacular than those of a few years ago: but they are not less intellectually interesting, nor is an understanding of them less necessary in order to clear the approach to those more vital questions of the creation and apportionment of real wealth with which the other volumes of this series are concerned.

§ 2. A Definition of Money.   It is clearly desirable to arrive at an early understanding of what we mean by money.   There is no very general agreement upon this point; but as with so many other economic terms, it does not matter very much what meaning we adopt as long as we stick to it, or at any rate do not change it without being aware that we are doing so. In this book, the term money will be used to denote anything which is widely accepted in payment for goods, or in discharge of other kinds of business obligation.   If things which are intended to be money—the notes of certain Governments, for instance—cease to be widely accepted in discharge of obligations, they cease to function as money, and, from the point of view of the student at any rate, to *be* money.   On the other hand, if things which have not been hitherto considered as money, such as tobacco or cattle or tins of bully-beef, become widely accepted in discharge of obligations, they become, in our present sense, money.[1]

This property of being widely acceptable generally, though not always, involves another, namely, the property of being expressed in units, in terms of which it is common to reckon the value of all those goods and services which men are in the habit of exchanging with one another.   This is what the text-books on money mean to convey when they say that money is not only a 'medium of exchange' but a 'standard of value.'

[1] Of the beer in which in effect wages were partly paid in the Staffordshire coal-mines in the middle of the nineteenth century, a recent historian remarks: 'This currency was very popular and highly liquid, but it was issued to excess and difficult to store.' Fay, *Life and Labour in the Nineteenth Century*, p. 197.

But that statement as it stands does not quite fit in with the definition of money which we have chosen.   It is not necessary that everything which is used as a medium of exchange should itself be also a standard of value, but only that it should be expressed in terms of something which *is* a standard of value. For instance, John Smith's cheques may be widely accepted in discharge of his obligations, and are therefore rightly regarded, according to the definition which we have chosen, as money: and Bank of England five-pound notes are universally accepted in Great Britain in discharge of obligations, and are certainly money.   But nobody reckons his income or conducts his business dealings in terms of John Smith's cheques or even of Bank of England notes: people reckon their incomes and conduct their transactions in terms of the pounds sterling of which John Smith's cheques and Bank of England notes are expressed as multiples.

Money then is anything which is widely acceptable in discharge of obligations: but a thing will not as a rule be widely acceptable for this purpose unless it is expressed as a multiple of some unit which is regarded as a measure or standard of the value of things in general.   This conception of a 'standard of value' raises some difficulties, to which we must return later: and we must also postpone for the present a consideration of the different *kinds* of money which exist, and of the ways in which various money systems are built up out of them.   Meanwhile what there is to be said applies to *all* money defined as we have defined it.

§ 3. The Advantage of Money to the Consumer.   The next question for our consideration is 'What is the point of using money?'   We have become so accustomed to the use of money that it requires a little exercise of imagination to realise how much we owe to it.   But over large parts of the world in recent years people have been deprived of the advantages of a sound system of money, and have found out how inconvenient and even paralysing the consequences may be.

The first great achievement of money is that it enables man

as consumer to generalise his purchasing power, and to make his claims on society in the form which suits him best. If there were no money, people would have to be paid for their services in kind; and whether they were strictly rationed, or whether they were allowed to help themselves to an unlimited extent, in either case there would be waste. For in the former case they would be encouraged to take more of certain goods and services, and forced to take less of others, than they really require; and in the latter case they would be tempted to be extravagant all round. The existence of a monetary economy helps society to discover what people want and how much they want it, and so to decide what shall be produced and in what quantities, and to make the best use of its limited productive power. And it helps each member of society to ensure that the *means* of enjoyment to which he has access yield him the greatest amount of *actual* enjoyment which is within his reach—it gives him the chance of not surfeiting himself with bus rides, or stinting himself unduly of the countenance of Charlie Chaplin.

How fully he avails himself of this opportunity depends on his aptitude for judging accurately of the relative amounts of enjoyment which different ways of spending a penny or a shilling would afford him, and on his strength of mind in acting on his judgment. Some people exploit to the full this opportunity of 'making the most of their income': others settle down to a comfortable habit of customary expenditure, and regard immunity from excessive brain-wear about the spending of money, and from the keeping of meticulous accounts, as worth some leakage of material enjoyment. To waste satisfaction by 'going on the burst' may even be itself a source of satisfaction. But in any case man values highly this privilege of spending his money income, that is of taking his real income, as he pleases—how highly you may see if you read the story of the fight against the truck system of paying wages, or watch the faces of an engaged couple as they open the parcel containing their seventeenth writing-case.

There are indeed some services, such as the use of the roads, which we all of us receive without making specific payment. Further, in some callings, such as the Army or domestic service, a more extensive payment in kind is generally recognised to be for the convenience of everybody concerned: and those who have given rein to their fancy in delineating the ideal economic society of the future have often contemplated some system of doles or rationing for the distribution of those staple commodities of which all human beings stand in need. But since even such an ideal society would not be likely to be infinitely rich, the total claim which any individual could make upon it would still have to be limited: and since individual tastes and requirements would presumably continue to differ, people would still have to be given a certain amount of latitude and discretion with regard to the form in which they presented part at any rate of their claims.   In other words, money of some kind—certificates, that is to say, of a general title to real income, to be interpreted and particularised by the individual—would have to persist.   The need for money then seems to be fundamental, if a given volume of productive power—a given poise of mankind in his relations with nature—is to be made to yield the greatest harvest of individual satisfaction which it is capable of yielding.

§ **4. The Advantage of Money to the Producer.**   The second great achievement of money is that it enables man as producer to concentrate his attention on his own job, and so to add more effectively to the general flow of goods and services which constitutes the real income of society.   Historically, the process of 'commutation' of payments in kind into payments in money is found to be very closely bound up with the process of 'differentiation' of various crafts and occupations: and logically the intimate connection between the two is not difficult to understand.   The specialisation and division of labour on which our economic structure is founded would be impossible if every man had to spend a large part of his time and energies in bartering his products for the materials of his industry and the goods which he requires for his own consumption.

This is especially true of the system of large-scale 'capitalistic' production which is dominant to-day. The various forms which this system takes are discussed in more detail in another volume: but for our present purposes it is sufficiently accurate to describe it as one under which a large number of workmen work for wages under the orders of a 'capitalist,' who is responsible for the disposal of their joint product, and who allocates a share of the proceeds to the individual workmen. Now it would as a rule be intolerable from a business point of view if every large 'capitalist'—say an ironmaster or the managing director of a railway company—had to lay in a store of all the things his workmen are likely to want and to dole them out to them. In certain conditions indeed, as experience shows, a partial arrangement of this kind may be put into force, either because it is a source of illicit profit to the 'capitalist' (as under the old truck system), or because it furnishes a special incentive to the workman (as in the case of the special butter wages allowed in 1919 to coal miners in Germany), or because (as in domestic service) it is manifestly to the convenience of both parties. But speaking generally it is far simpler, and is indeed the only practicable course, for the 'capitalist' to pay his workmen money wages, which they accept in the confident expectation of being able to obtain with them the things which they require. The existence of money then seems to be a necessary condition for any great development of the division of labour not merely as between those who follow different crafts, but as between those who plan and initiate and control and those who do the day-work of the world. Whether this is a thing for money to be proud of is of course another matter: all that is urged here is that in so far as the capitalistic system of industry has been an indispensable instrument of material progress, money has been so too.

The third great achievement of money is closely allied to the second. It consists in this, that money immensely facilitates the making of loans and payments in advance of all kinds. Wage payments, which have been mentioned above, are in essence one form of such payment in advance.   The 'capitalist' will not be able to dispose finally of his product till it is in a finished state: but the workmen engaged on the preliminary stages must be enabled to live meanwhile, and money facilitates arrangements being made for this.   The making of advances by one kind of business man to another is also rendered much easier by the existence of money: so is the investment or loaning of its savings by the general public.   Lending and saving mean in the last resort the lending and saving of real things, and they may exist without money: but so long at any rate as we rely for them upon individuals, they would be very cumbrous and difficult to arrange on a large scale without the aid of money.   So for this reason too the existence of money seems to be essential to our modern system of production, which rests so largely upon the willingness of one man to transfer command over goods to another, in the expectation of being repaid either by that other or by some third party at a future date.

§ **5. The Monetary Veil over Lending and Saving.**   But this third great achievement of a monetary economy is also one of its two great drawbacks and dangers.   For it means that the operations of lending and saving are shrouded behind a monetary veil, and that what really happens behind the veil is sometimes quite different from what appears to take place upon the surface.   Sometimes the monetary system works in such a way that the willingness of people to lend and save is rendered abortive and runs to waste: so that men stand idle in thousands although other men are willing and able to do the saving which is necessary to set them to work.   A kind of paralysis creeps over the monetary machine, and leads to industrial stagnation and decay.

But at other times the machine operates in such a way as to lead to an *apparent* lending of things which turn out not really to exist at all.   Thus when there is a 'boom' in the constructional trades—steel, shipbuilding, engineering and the rest—'capitalists' in these trades bid for the services of workpeople by offering them plentiful money wages. As was explained above, these wages are really in the nature of an advance, backed by the estimates made by the 'capitalists' of the value which society will set on the buildings and ships and so forth which are in process of production. But what the workman wants these money advances for is to obtain the necessaries and conventional comforts of his life: and under a money-system there is no guarantee that these are being turned out as fast as the money wages are being handed over. Hence we may get a state of affairs when industry is active and wages high, but the necessaries of life are scarce; and then there is outcry and unrest. If every business man had to make arrangements himself for feeding and clothing and amusing his employees before he embarked on any venture, as he might have to do if he were building a railway, say over the Andes, hundreds of miles from civilisation, such maladjustments would not occur; but of course industrial progress would be very slow and difficult. As it is, the ease with which advances of every kind can be made in money oils the wheels of material progress: but the result is that people tend to confuse the pieces of money, which are mere certificates of a right to draw goods which may not even exist, with the goods themselves and to lay up all sorts of trouble and disillusionment for themselves. Adam Smith once compared money to a road, over which all the produce of a district passes to market, but which does not itself produce a single blade of anything. Nobody would be so foolish as to expect to eat a road: yet man is always being surprised afresh by the discovery that he cannot eat money, as the Turks are said to be surprised afresh each year by the advent of winter.

§ 6. Monetary Instability and the Distribution of Wealth. The second great drawback about money is closely bound up with the first, and turns on the fact that its value does not, even in ordinary times, remain perfectly stable, and in times of disturbance is liable to very great variation. We shall have to examine more carefully in a moment what we mean by this phrase 'the value of money'; for the present we may define it provisionally as the power of money to purchase the things people want. Now we should not be wise at this early stage of our study to take it for granted that we want the value of money under all conditions to remain perfectly unchanging; but we shall not run much risk in accepting the suggestion of common sense that large and undesigned changes in this value are likely to be disastrous, and that even more moderate variation carries on the face of it certain disadvantages. Let us take then a preliminary glance at how the matter works.

All of us, from landowner to labourer, are enabled to live because other people want our services, if we take that word in an extended sense to include the use of our possessions: and if the power of other people's money to buy our services always varied in exactly the same degree as the power of our money to buy other people's services, there is no reason why these variations in the purchasing power of money should matter to any of us. But in fact that is not the way things happen. Some people sell their services on conditions which are fixed, by legal contract or by the force of custom, for a long time ahead in terms of money: other people are easily enabled or forced, as the case may be, to bring about alterations in the prices of the services they sell. The former group of people are clearly benefited by a rise and injured by a fall in the value of money: for in the former case they receive a greater and in the latter case a smaller power of command than they expected over the things which they require. The latter group of people tend to gain by a fall and to lose by a rise in the value of money: for they make use, whether for purposes of further production or for their own enjoyment, of the services of people whose money rewards are fixed, while their own money rewards are variable. Any change therefore, however slight, in the value of money, so long as it is not perfectly foreseen, leads to a certain redistribution of the real income of society between these two groups of persons. And if, as happened in many European countries in the years after the war, there occurs a violent and prolonged fall in the value of money, many of the former group are likely to be reduced to utter penury and ruin.

Before the war it was possible to lay down fairly definitely the classes of which each of these two groups was composed. Broadly speaking, the former comprised wage-earners, professional people (such as Government officials and schoolmasters), and those who had made loans, whether to Governments or to industrial companies, at a fixed rate of money interest. The latter group comprised the 'business classes,' those, that is, who derived an income from venturing and planning and controlling the production and sale of goods: for their money expenses for the hire of labour and capital remained relatively fixed, while their money incomes fluctuated with the prices of the things they sold. At the present day this generalisation is still in the main true, but the situation has been greatly complicated by the increased power of certain sections of Labour and by the piecemeal interventions of the State. The violent fall in the value of money between 1914 and 1920, and its almost equally violent rise in the immediately ensuing years, led, even in England, to a great and often arbitrary redistribution of income, not only between different social and industrial classes, but between different persons in the same class. If the reader chances to be a railway shareholder or a shipwright, he will probably hold that he had been damaged on the balance by the changes which have occurred; if he is a motor-manufacturer or a railway porter he will probably admit to himself, though not to the world, that things have not worked out so badly. And his attitude towards future changes also will depend on his calling as well as on his general industrial status.

§ 7. Monetary Instability and the Creation of Wealth. But this is not all. If the effects of the instability of the value of money were exercised only on the way in which wealth is shared, they might not be of such fundamental importance: for though the consequent changes might not bear much relation to social justice, they would not necessarily diminish

the total economic welfare of society, and might even substantially increase it. The loss of some would be the gain of others: and the others might on the whole be the more necessitous and even the more deserving. But in fact any violent or prolonged exhibition of instability in the value of money affects not only the distribution but also the creation of real wealth: for it threatens to undermine the basis of contract and business expectation on which our economic order is built up. That order is largely based on the institution of *contract*—on the fact, that is, that people enter into voluntary but binding agreements with one another to perform certain actions at a future date, for a remuneration which is fixed here and now in terms of money. And a violent or prolonged change in the value of money saps the confidence with which people make or accept undertakings of this nature. It is of course conceivable that contracts should be framed in terms of something other than money: it is even conceivable, or so some people assure us, that society should come to rely on some other method than free contract, such as the fiat of an industrial autocrat or the promptings of spontaneous benevolence, for getting its work done. But so long as reliance on the method of contract as we know it persists, so long are the vagaries of the value of money a potential cause of disaster.

None of us, however, can reduce the whole of his working life within the sphere of definite and formal contract: for the rest we live by calculation, expectation, faith. And these too are threatened, both by the instability of the value of money and by the attempts, necessarily impromptu and incomplete, which are made by society to minimise its evil results. For society, even when scrupulously regardful of contract, cannot always afford to be very tender towards more indefinite expectations. It was, for instance, inevitable, though not altogether fortunate, that during the war those 'capitalists' in Great Britain who were concerned with the rendering of the most indisputably necessary services—the provision of coal, of railway transport, of house-room—should be singled out for the most drastic attentions of the State and the trade unions.

The resulting situation was indeed somewhat paradoxical. Just as the more obviously useful and important the industry in which a workman is employed, the more odium he incurs if he strikes to better his position, because he is 'holding up society to ransom'; so the more obviously useful and important the direction in which a man had invested his savings, or exercised his brain-power, or shouldered the burden of risk, the greater precautions did the State seem to take that the fall in the value of money should operate to his hurt. *Noblesse oblige*: but it is not altogether astonishing if those thus put under obligation sometimes grew peevish and threatened to refuse to play. Thus monetary disease and improvised remedy alike strike at those roots of undefined but not unreasonable anticipation, from which the tree of industry is still expected to derive so large a proportion of its sustenance.

Nor is it only, or chiefly, through a falling value of money that expectations are thus frustrated and fruitful activity discouraged. Still more obviously does a prolonged rise in the value of money, by injuring and disheartening those who are in charge of the commercial and industrial machines, retard the creation of wealth and play havoc with individual lives.

For let us consider how it operates. A downward swoop of the level of prices reveals like a flare a line of struggling figures, caught in their own commitments as in a barbed-wire entanglement. Not one of them can tell what or how soon the end will be. For a while each strives, with greater or less effectiveness, to maintain the price of his own particular wares; but sooner or later he succumbs to the stream, and tries to unload his holdings while he can, lest worse should befall. And right from the start he has taken the one step open to him; he has cut off the new stream of enmeshing goods, and passed the word to his predecessor not to add to his burden. So the manufacturer finds the outlet for his wares narrowing from a cormorant's gullet to a needle's eye; and he too takes what steps occur to him. If he is old and wily and has made his pile he retires from business for a season, and goes for a sea-voyage or into the House of Commons. If he is young and ambitious or idealistic he keeps the ball rolling and the flag flying as best he can. If he is an average sort of manufacturer he explains that while he adheres to his previous opinion that the finance of his business is no concern of the working-classes, yet just so much financial knowledge as to see the absurdity of the existing trade union rate is a thing which any workman should possess. In any case,

> Early or late,
> He stoops to fate,

and restricts in greater or less degree the output of his product. Thus two things happen which (it is believed) cause much merriment among the inhabitants of other planets. The world deliberately adopts a standard of comfort lower than that which its natural resources and its capital equipment place within its reach, cutting off its nose, as it were, to spite its face. And men trained and willing to work find no work to do, and tramp the streets with the parrot-cries of journalists about increased output ringing in their ears, and growing rancour in their hearts.

Thus money, which is a source of so many blessings to mankind, becomes also, unless we can control it, a source of peril and confusion. But in order to form sensible views about how to control it, we must first understand it. The next three chapters of this book will be occupied with a broad survey of the forces determining the value of money: the two which follow with two rather special topics bearing on the same matter. Not till the last two chapters of the book shall we be ready to discuss the lofty theme of monetary policy.

CHAPTER II

THE VALUE OF MONEY

'When *I* use a word,' Humpty Dumpty said in rather a scornful tone, 'it means just what I choose it to mean—neither more nor less.'

'The question is,' said Alice, 'whether you *can* make words mean different things.'

'The question is,' said Humpty Dumpty, 'which is to be master—that's all.'

Through the Looking-glass

I. What is Meant by the Value of Money

§ 1. A Definition of the Value of Money. By the value of money we mean something exactly analogous to what we mean by the value of anything else, say bread or cloth: that is to say, we mean the amount of things in general which will be given in exchange for a unit of money. But a difficulty arises from the fact that we are in the habit, for the sake of convenience, of expressing the value of bread or cloth in terms of money, whereas obviously we cannot express the value of money in terms of itself. There is therefore no way in which we could express accurately the value of a pound sterling except by enumerating one by one all the different articles which it would buy: and this would clearly be too tedious for words. There are, however, as we shall see in a moment, ways—though not entirely satisfactory ways—of expressing *differences* in the value of a pound sterling between one time or place and another: and that is all that in practice we want to do. But in any case the difficulty is one of expression: it does not mean that when we speak of the value

14

of money we are using the word value with any different meaning from that which we attach to it in speaking of the value of bread or cloth.

There is, however, a further difficulty. What exactly do we mean by 'things in general'? All people use money in spending their incomes, that is to say in buying the flow of goods and services which enter into ordinary consumption. But the real *income* or *output* of the country consists only partly of such consumption goods and services; it comprises also new capital goods, such as buildings and machinery, which are bought by business men. Further, business men use money also for other purposes, such as the purchase of raw materials, the hire of labour, and the exchange of *existing* capital goods such as land and houses. When, therefore, we speak of the value of money, we must be clear whether we are thinking of its value in terms only of the goods and services which enter into ordinary consumption, or of its value in terms of all the newly created things which make up the country's real income or output, or of its value in terms of all the things of whatever kind which are exchanged with its aid. We may call these three things its 'consumption value,' its 'income-value' and its 'transaction-value' respectively; and it will be well to state here, though we shall not make use of the idea till a much later stage, that there is yet a *fourth* thing which has particular claims on our attention, namely the '*labour-value*' of money, that is to say the amount of labour of a given quality which a unit of money will command.

§ 2. Changes in the Value of Money. The measurement of changes in the value of money has become a matter of considerable practical interest. Most English people permitted themselves now and again to endorse some such estimate of the extent of war-time changes as was conveyed in the reproachful but nebulous statements, that 'a pound is only worth eight shillings,' or that 'half a crown only goes as far as a shilling ought to go.' And a good many English people, notably civil servants and railwaymen, still find their money

3

incomes definitely varying in accordance with some official estimate of changes in the value of money. But unfortunately the subject is also one of considerable theoretical difficulty. It is indeed the chosen paradise and playground of the mathematicians, who have expended untold ingenuity upon it. One distinguished mathematical economist has gone so far as to conduct a kind of competitive examination of forty-four algebraical formulæ of increasing complexity, representing different methods of measuring the changes in the value of money, to which he has allotted marks in accordance with their possession of certain qualifications; and some of them make a very poor show indeed. Nevertheless some of the difficulties of the subject are very instructive, and are also implicit in the criticisms which the ordinary man is apt to make of current estimates: and it is therefore worth while to bestow a little attention upon them.

The problem of course is to build up, out of the figures showing the changes in the prices of particular things, an index-number, as it is called, of general prices, which shall show at a glance the change in the value of money. A rise in this index-number will indicate a corresponding fall in the value of money—will indicate, that is, that a smaller bundle of things in general will be obtained in exchange for a given unit of money: and a fall in the index-number will indicate a corresponding rise in the value of money.

We may pass over lightly the *practical* difficulties in the way of constructing such an index-number; for they are sufficiently obvious. It is not always easy to get accurate figures of prices, except for certain staple commodities sold wholesale, though it is now being done with much greater success than it used to be. Again, it is not easy to be sure that the things whose prices we are comparing are the same thing: a bus ride during which you sit down is not the same thing as a bus ride during which you have to keep on giving up your seat. But it will be more profitable to devote our attention to the more fundamental difficulties involved by the construction of an index-number of general prices.

First, then, before constructing our index-number we must be clear what purpose it is to serve. If it is to show the changes in the value of money in the most general sense, it must include all the things which are the subjects of exchange in the economic world, including land and houses and securities and so forth. If, on the other hand, we want it to indicate the cost of living for ordinary people, we shall leave out these things, and include only such goods and services as enter into ordinary consumption. Again, even so we must be clear *whose* cost of living it is, the change in which we are estimating. We must not, for instance, hastily apply a figure for the change in the cost of living among the working-classes to express the change in the cost of living in college at Cambridge. And in any case our figure cannot be accurate for persons of widely different tastes, even if they live in the same social environment. The value of money may have changed in widely different degree to the heavy drinker and the teetotaller. The person to whom our index-number applies is at best an abstraction: all we can do is to make him as representative as possible.

§ **3. Difficulties of Measurement.** Secondly, when we have decided what things to include, the question arises as to how we are to combine the price movements of the several things in order to obtain our final index-number. The obvious suggestion is that we should take the average of the several percentage price changes and regard that as the percentage change in general prices. But a simple example will show that this suggestion conceals a trap.[1] Let us suppose, to simplify matters, that we can regard two articles—say bread and beer—as sufficient to furnish us with a good index-number; and that we are comparing—it must be emphasised that the example is purely imaginary—conditions in the years 1900 and 1910. Suppose that during this period the price of bread was doubled and the price of beer was halved. Then if we

[1] For the whole of the following discussion, cf. Pigou, *Economics of Welfare,* Part I, Chap. V.

represent the price of each in 1900 as 100, the price of bread in 1910 was 200 and the price of beer was 50. The sum of their prices is seen to have risen from 200 to 250, and the *average* price—our 'index-number of general prices'—to have risen from 100 to 125. But if now we represent the price of each in 1910 as 100, the price of bread in 1900 appears as 50 and the price of beer as 200; so that the sum of their prices appears to have fallen between 1900 and 1910 from 250 to 200, and the average price to have fallen from 125 to 100. That is to say we get a *fall* of one-fifth instead of a *rise* of one-quarter in our 'index-number of general prices.' We thus get completely different results according to the year which we take as the starting-point of our calculations, or as the experts say as our *base*: and from the point of view of the historian there is obviously nothing particularly sacred about one year more than another.

For convenience of inspection this result is set out again in the following table:

	I		II	
	1900	1910	1900	1910
Bread . .	100	200	50	100
Beer . .	100	50	200	100
Sum . .	2)200	2)250	2)250	2)200
Average	100	125	125	100
		+25%	−20%	

Now some of the experts tell us that provided we include a sufficient number of articles in our index-number, the possibility of this kind of absurd result need not seriously disturb us: for the average movement of the prices of a large number of articles will show us correctly the direction of the movement of the general price-level, and will even show us its magnitude with as much accuracy as we want for practical purposes. But other experts tell us—and they are able to support their contention with striking examples—that this is too optimistic a view, and that such a simple index-number may lead us seriously wrong, especially if there have been great changes in prices and other conditions between the two years which are being compared.   It is of interest therefore to try to discover the cause of the absurd result which we reached just now, and to see whether it can be obviated.

A little reflection will show that the reason why we reached divergent results according to the year which we took as our base was that we were really comparing different things in the two cases.   In the first case we were following the fortunes of a combination of things consisting of the amount of bread which could be bought for 100 units of money in 1900 + the amount of beer which could be bought for 100 units of money in 1900.   In the second case we were following the fortunes of a combination consisting of the amount of bread which could be bought for 100 units of money in 1910 + the amount of beer which could be bought for 100 units of money in 1910.

Let us make one more supposition in order to get a definite example.   Suppose that in 1900 a loaf of bread and a pint of beer each cost 6d.; and the combination of the two therefore cost 1s.   Then in 1910 a loaf of bread cost 1s. and a pint of beer cost 3d., and the combination of the two cost 1s. 3d.: that is to say, the price of this particular combination— 1 loaf + 1 pint—had risen 25 per cent.   But now let us follow the fortunes of the price of the combination which could be obtained by spending 6d. on each of the two articles, not in 1900, but in 1910: this combination is clearly $\frac{1}{2}$ loaf of bread + 2 pints of beer.   In 1900 this combination cost 1s. 3d., whereas in 1910 it only cost 1s.; that is to say, the price of this particular combination fell in the period by 20 per cent.   Both our measures of the general price change are accurate, but each of them is accurate only for one particular combination of the articles included.   The combination in our first example is that which could be obtained by spending an equal sum— whether a penny or a pound makes no difference whatever—on each of the articles in the first of the two years compared; the combination in our second example is that which could be obtained by spending an equal sum on each of the articles in the second year. Both these combinations are clearly quite arbitrary.

§ **4. Provisional Solution.** Let us see then if we can find a combination which is not arbitrary. An obvious suggestion is that we should take the combination which is actually the subject of exchange in the year which we select as base. For instance, if we are making an index-number to throw light on changes in the cost of living for the working classes, we can follow the fortunes of a combination consisting of so much of each of the articles in question as was actually consumed by the normal working-class family in our base year. This—or something like it—is what is actually done by the index-number which has attracted most attention from the British public since the war—the so-called Ministry of Labour index-number of the cost of living (we shall see in a moment that the popular name for it is not accurate), which has been the basis for the sliding scale of railway wages. If it is said that that number has risen by 65 per cent since July, 1914, what is meant is that the average working-class family would have to pay 65 per cent more now than in July, 1914, for the collection of articles which it is presumed to have been in the habit of consuming in July, 1914.

Have we then obtained a satisfactory measure of changes in general prices? Again, alas! the answer is No. So long as there have not been violent changes between the two dates compared, the measure may be fairly satisfactory; but if there have, it is not. For people will probably have increased their consumption of those things which have fallen most, or risen least, in price: and they will probably have cut down their consumption of those things which have fallen least, or risen most, in price. And there may be—in time of war there were —other causes of disturbance to consumption besides changes in relative prices. It may even be that old articles have vanished from the market altogether, and new articles been introduced. A generation which knows not butter may have supplanted a generation which knew not margarine. In such circumstances it becomes merely of archæological interest to know what has happened to the price of the combination consumed in the base year: for the combination consumed in the later years is completely different. It is for this reason that it is inaccurate to speak of the Ministry of Labour figure mentioned above as a 'cost of living' index, and that people often vaguely feel that there is something unsatisfactory about it. That figure does not mean that (for instance) it actually cost the working-class family 150 per cent more to obtain food, clothing, and so forth in June, 1920, than it did in July, 1914, but that it *would have* cost it 150 per cent more in June, 1920, to obtain the exact collection of things customarily bought in July, 1914, a collection which it would not have been physically possible for the family to buy in June, 1920 (for instance as regards sugar), even if it had wished to. The tendency still persists in economic matters to attribute a peculiar sanctity to the year 1914; all sorts of people who were very discontented at the time tend to look back to it now as having been in some sense the 'normal' or standard year for all time: and so long as this sentiment is general there is something to be said for following with interest the changes in price of combinations of things consumed in 1914. But the time will come when this conception will be obsolete: by about 1950, for instance, it may be scarcely more interesting to know the price of the combination of things consumed by the working-class family in 1914 than to know what the price would be in England of the combination of things habitually consumed by Chinamen.

One rough way of meeting the difficulty would be to take the percentage price change of the combination consumed at the first date, and the percentage price change of the combination consumed at the second date, and to strike an average between them; and to treat this average as a measure of the change in general prices. But there are all sorts of other mathematical devices for securing the same end, into which we need not enter. The chief point is to understand the essential difficulty involved, and not to expect any index-number to be completely water-tight and truthful.

It is worth pointing out that an exactly similar difficulty is met in attempting to compare the value of money in different *places*. For instance, a Board of Trade enquiry into the relative cost of living in England and Germany some years before the war showed that the combination of things ordinarily consumed by an English workman cost about 20 per cent more in Germany than in England, while the combination of things ordinarily consumed by a German workman only cost about 10 per cent more. And an attempt to compare the value of money in two countries with widely different civilisations—say England and the Cannibal Islands—would be practically meaningless: for the combination of things to be taken into account would be completely different, including for each country things—such as motor cars perhaps and missionaries —which nobody in the other country either could buy, or would buy if he could.

The conclusion then is that neither in practice nor perhaps even in theory is it possible to measure accurately changes in the value of money. Nevertheless there is no doubt that the value of money does change, and, if sufficient care is taken, measures accurate enough for some practical purposes can be found and used. Most important countries now publish an index-number of retail prices, which can be taken as a measure of changes in the consumption-value of money. For an indication of changes in its transaction-value we have to be content for the most part with index-numbers of the prices of commodities at wholesale, such as that of the British Board of Trade (150 commodities) and the American Bureau of Labour (550 commodities). Most important modern index-numbers are 'weighted'—that is to say, an attempt is made to allow for the relative importance of the different articles, generally in accordance with the relative amount spent on them in some selected period; and when information is available this selected period is altered so as to bring the weights as nearly as possible up to date. The Bureau of Labour for instance has taken to recalculating its weights every two years.

II. How the Value of Money is Determined

§ 5. Resemblances between Money and Other Things. We are now in a position to approach the question of the *forces* by which the value of money is *determined*, as distinct from the question of the *devices* by which changes in it can be *measured*. This is the most difficult and fundamental question that we have to face, and we shall not be done with it for several chapters. To make it manageable for ourselves, we must tackle it piecemeal. In this chapter we must be content if we can set in order the main forces which, in a period of comparative stability, are steadily at work to keep the value of money none other than what it is. Our apparatus, that is to say, will be more useful for comparing broadly the value of money in, say, the eighteen-nineties, in the pre-war decade, and at the present day, than for explaining its behaviour during a period of rapid change such as in the years 1914 to 1921. It will resemble rather a telescope used for picking up in succession two or more ships riding at anchor, than a pair of field-glasses used for watching the progress of a race.

Once more we can keep on the right lines if we start by remembering that money is only one of many economic things. Its value therefore is primarily determined by exactly the same two factors as determine the value of any other thing, namely, the conditions of demand for it, and the quantity of it available. In following out this idea, it is open to us to pursue either of two courses. We can fix our attention either on the *stock* of money in existence at a given *point* of time, or on the *flow* of money being used during a given *period* of time. Each of these procedures has its own advantages, and it will be well to be familiar with both of them before we have done; but since the main purpose of money is to be used, the latter procedure is perhaps that which comes more naturally to the ordinary man. Let us start then by fixing our attention on money on the wing, as opposed to money sitting. And by the value of money let us mean for the present its transaction-value—its value, that is, in terms of all the goods and services which it is used to purchase.

Looking at the matter in this way, we see that the conditions of demand for money consist in the total volume of business transactions of all kinds which has to be performed within a given time with the aid of money. The volume of business transactions to be performed may increase for various reasons. Perhaps the flow of finished goods and services which have to be distributed among the community for final consumption increases. Or perhaps, whether owing to an outburst of speculative activity or to a change in the organisation of industry, raw materials such as cotton and wheat come to change hands more often before taking on their final form of shirts and loaves of bread. Or perhaps for some reason the exchange of capital goods such as houses and securities becomes more active. In any case, an increase in the volume of transactions means an increase in the demand for money. And similarly a decrease in the volume of transactions means a decrease in the demand for money.

But *given the conditions of demand for money*, its value depends on the quantity of it available. If fewer units were available, there would be more work for each of them to do: each of them would have to exchange for a larger volume of other things—its value, as we have defined it, would be greater than it actually is. If more units of money were available, each of them would have to exchange for a smaller volume of things—its value would be less than it actually is. If we pursue our analysis to the bitter end, we shall be forced to admit that if even *one* unit of money were withdrawn from the quantity actually available, there would be some slight tendency for more work to fall upon the others, and for their value to rise. The value of each unit of money is what it is because there are just so many units, and neither more nor less, available: and the value of *every* unit of money is equal to the value of *any* unit among them which we can conceive of as being suddenly abolished.

Readers of the first volume of this series will readily see, therefore, that in this also the value of money resembles that of other things—that *given the conditions of demand*, it depends on the total number of units available, and is equal to the value of any such unit that we choose to conceive of as being suddenly abstracted.

§ 6. Differences between Money and Other Things.

We may now pass on to consider two respects in which the value of money is determined differently from the value of other things. The first respect is very important indeed. The value of bread is not only an expression of the bundle of things in general which can be obtained in exchange for a loaf of bread: it is also in some degree a measure of the usefulness, or enjoyment-yielding power, of a loaf of bread. If one of the available loaves were destroyed, there would be a corresponding loss in real economic welfare. Can we say the same about money?

From one point of view we can. If one unit of money were suddenly abolished, the possessor of the particular unit selected for abolition would clearly be the poorer. Nobody who has ever lost a sixpence through a crack in the floor will dispute this. But it is by no means obvious that the world as a whole would be impoverished in the same degree: for the command over real things surrendered by the loser of the sixpence is not abolished, but passes automatically to the rest of the community whose sixpences will now buy more. If indeed there were a large and simultaneous loss or destruction of money, society might easily find itself hampered in the conduct of its business, and the consequent check to exchange and production might lead to a serious decrease in its real economic welfare. But the fact remains that the value of money is (within limits) a measure of the usefulness of any one unit of money to its possessor, but not to society as a whole: while the value of bread is also a measure (within limits) of the *social* usefulness of any one loaf of bread. And the reason for this peculiarity about money is the fact that nobody generally speaking wants it except for the sake of the control which it gives over other things.

The second respect in which money is peculiar as regards the determination of its value is closely allied to the first: and while it is less important, it has attracted more attention. *Given the conditions of demand for money*, the relation between its value and the quantity of it available is of this peculiar kind; the larger the number of units available, the smaller, in exactly the same proportion, is the value of each unit. A moment's reflection will carry conviction that this must be true. If there is a certain volume of things to be exchanged, and if each of them is to change hands a certain number of times: then, if the quantity of money available were halved, there would be exactly twice as much work for each unit of money to do—each unit would have to pass in exchange for twice as great a volume of things in general. If the quantity of money available were doubled, there would be exactly half as much work for each unit to do—each unit would have to pass in exchange for half as great a volume of things in general. To use the correct arithmetical term, given the conditions of demand for money, its value *varies inversely* as the quantity available, or in other words the 'general level of prices' *varies directly* as the quantity of money available.

If, however, we are to avoid drawing false inferences from this interesting peculiarity of money, we must look a little more closely into the phrase 'the quantity of money available.' We decided, it will be remembered, to fix our attention for the present on the *flow* of money on to the markets during a given period of time—let us say a week. But during that week some of the pieces of money in existence will not be available for work; they may be holiday-making in my pocket, or taking a prolonged rest-cure in the bank, or even being 'cooled a long age in the deep-delved earth.' On the other hand, some will be available twice or thrice or many times, and will be used in one short week to discharge a number of quite separate transactions. Some pieces of money are very agile, like pieces of scandal, and skip easily from one person to another: others are like an old lady buying a railway ticket—one would think that they had lost the power of locomotion altogether. This truth is often expressed by saying that we must take account not only of the total quantity of money, but also of its average 'velocity of circulation.' And though we have found it convenient to approach it by a different route, it is precisely analogous to the truth that in estimating the demand for money we must take into account not only the volume of goods to be disposed of within a given time, but also the frequency with which each of them changes hands.

Here is a little story[1] to illustrate this conception of the velocity of circulation of money. On Derby Day two men, Bob and Joe, invested in a barrel of beer, and set off to Epsom with the intention of selling it retail on the racecourse at 6d. a pint, the proceeds to be shared equally between them. On the way Bob, who had one threepenny-bit left in the world, began to feel a great thirst, and drank a pint of the beer, paying Joe 3d. as his share of the market price. A little later Joe yielded to the same desire, and drank a pint of beer, returning the 3d. to Bob. The day was hot, and before long Bob was thirsty again, and so, a little later, was Joe. When they arrived at Epsom, the 3d. was back in Bob's pocket, and each had discharged in full his debts to the other: but the beer was all gone. One single threepenny-bit had performed a volume of transactions which would have required many shillings if the beer had been sold to the public in accordance with the original intention.

If we are interested, not in the 'transaction-value' of money, but in its 'income-value'—its value in terms of the goods and services which form part of real income or output—we can adopt the same method of approach. But in this case the velocity of circulation of money will mean, not the average number of times each piece of money is spent for any purpose whatsoever, but the average number of times it is spent in purchase of the goods and services which form part of real income or output, during the week or other period of time in

[1] Adapted from Edgeworth, *Economic Journal*, 1919, p. 329.

question. This 'income-velocity' of circulation of money is naturally much smaller than its 'transaction-velocity.'

§ 7. **The Public's Demand for Money.** We have now reached an answer which is definite so far as it goes. But if we are of an enquiring turn of mind, we shall still be very far from content. And the first question we shall ask is, What determines the velocity of circulation? Why is it that in any given country at any given time money is circulating at such and such a speed, and not either more rapidly or more slowly? The asking of this question gives us a convenient opportunity for giving our minds a healthy shake-up and approaching the whole question afresh, fixing our attention this time on money sitting instead of on money on the wing. And since at the end of the last section we turned our thoughts to the income-value instead of the transaction-value of money, let us for the moment keep them there, and see how we are to express the forces determining the income-value of money when by the quantity of money available we have decided to mean, not the flow of money on to the markets during a given period, but the stock of money in existence at a point of time. We shall find that we now have to change somewhat the meaning of our phrase 'the conditions of demand,' and to adopt an interpretation of those words which is at first sight rather more difficult than the one we have adopted so far, but which is really more in accordance with what we ordinarily mean by the word 'demand,' because it brings us into touch with the operations of human minds, instead of attaching the notion of demand to a stream of inanimate commodities.

It will be readily granted that the ordinary person likes to keep to his hand a little pool of money, partly for the sake of convenience in conducting the ordinary business of life and partly as a margin to fall back on in unforeseen contingencies. He may thus be said, without straining language, to exercise a 'demand' for money: but whereas his demand for bread clothes itself in the form of an offer of money, it is obvious that his demand for money itself cannot be expressed in terms

of money.   A little reflection will show, however, that it can
be expressed in terms of the real things—food and travel and
so forth, and also, in the case of the business man, nice new
buildings and machinery—the purchase of which he forgoes
in order to enjoy instead the practical convenience and peace
of mind yielded him by his pool of money.   If we are puzzled
as to how we can measure a demand which consists of such a
hotch-potch of diverse elements, we must remind ourselves
that this is only another aspect of the problem which has been
discussed in the first part of this chapter in connection with
index-numbers of prices, and that the rough solutions there
obtained are applicable to our present difficulty as well.   Without further discussion of it therefore we can go on to lay down
that an individual's demand for money consists in the real
aggregate value, in terms of the goods and services in which
he is interested, of his money pool.

Now in the case of every individual this pool of real value
which is as it were crystallised for him in the shape of money
can be expressed as a proportion of his annual real income—
that is, of the flow of goods and services which his annual
money income gives him the right to command.   This proportion will be different for different individuals according to
the nature of their habits and employment, nor is it likely in
the case of any individual to be the same at every moment.
If we take for instance the simple case of a labourer who is
paid 35s. once a week, and spends the whole of his income
regularly at the rate of 5s. a day, his proportion, while it varies
during the week all the way between zero and 100 per cent of
his weekly income, works out on the average at 50 per cent of
that income.   On the other hand we should be surprised if
we found a civil servant on £1000 a year with as little as half
a week's income, say £10, on the average in the bank.   But
taking the country as a whole at any given time, we can express
its demand for money—that is, the real value of its money-
supply—as a proportion of its real national income—that is
of the flow of goods and services becoming available during
the year for final purchase by its inhabitants.   To give a touch

of reality to our proceedings, it may be said at once that for
Great Britain that proportion seems to be about one-half.

On what then does the magnitude of this proportion depend?
It depends on the one hand, as has been said, on the convenience
and sense of security derived from the possession of a pool of
money, and on the other, on the strength of the alternative
attractions of increased consumption, or lucrative investment
in trade capital or in Government or industrial stocks, against
which these advantages have to be weighed up. Thus the
magnitude of the demand for money, like that of the demand
for bread, turns out to be the result of a process of individual
weighing-up of competing advantages *at the margin*: and the
reader of the first volume of this series will hail with delight
a new bond between money and other things. As to the
convenience of holding a money pool, the reader can amuse
himself by drawing up a list of the economic conditions and
habits which will be likely to render it great or small as the
case may be. He will find for instance that it will be greater
the less frequent are the intervals at which people discharge
their obligations, because in such circumstances more money
will be kept idling about at any one time. Thus, as the
example given above suggests, the demand for money will be
greater if people are paid quarterly salaries than if they are
paid weekly wages.

§ 8. **Money Sitting and Money on the Wing.** Now what is the
relation between the demand for money, in the sense in which
we have just been using those words, and the conception of
'velocity of circulation' which we used when we were studying
money on the wing? The answer is very simple. If people
want to keep ready to their hand a large pool of command over
goods and services, money will be kept hanging about and its
velocity of circulation will be small. If for any reason the
intensity of their desire to keep such a pool diminishes, they
will begin to spend their money faster, and its velocity of
circulation will increase. The proportion of their annual real
income over which people wish to keep command in the form

of money *is* the income-velocity of circulation of money per annum turned upside down. If, for instance, as has been suggested, that proportion for Great Britain is one-half, this *means* that in Great Britain each piece of money in existence is used on the average twice a year in purchase of the goods and services which form part of real income.

The reader will note with relief that the peculiarity which we found about money, namely, that given the conditions of demand for it its value varies inversely as the quantity available (p. 26), remains equally in evidence when we consider money as a stock and not as a flow. For if a person decides to keep ready to his hand enough money to purchase half the goods and services which his annual money-income entitles him to purchase, it makes no difference to him whether that stock takes the form of 100 units of money each of a given value, or of 200 units of money each of half that value. Given the community's 'demand for money,' in the sense explained in § 7, the aggregate value of the community's money-stock is determined, irrespective of the number of units of money of which it is composed.

For the benefit of those who have a passion for symmetry it may be added that the ideas which we have acquired from studying money sitting can be applied to the examination of the transaction-value of money as easily as to the examination of its income-value. We have only to substitute the notion of the proportion of their *annual real turnover* which people wish to have enough money at hand to conduct, for the notion of the proportion of annual real income which they wish to have enough money at hand to purchase. But since this refinement does not seem to lead us on to any new fruitful ideas, it will be left to the reader to play with it further or not as he desires.[1]

§ **9. Problems Ahead.** Let us now see exactly where we stand. So far our gymnastic exercises have all been designed to

---

[1] Those readers only who are helped rather than frightened by the use of symbols are invited to turn to App. A, I.

elucidating the proposition that the value of money, like that of other things, depends on the conditions of demand for it and on the quantity of it available. Broadly speaking, the sitting money exercise is the more useful for enabling us to understand the underlying psychological forces determining the value of money; while the money on the wing exercise is the more useful for equipping us to watch with understanding the actual processes by which in real life the prices of goods and services change—for reminding us that the quantity of money and the quantity of goods do not affect the price-level by some kind of occult planetary influence, but by modifying the capacity or willingness of human beings to buy or refrain from buying, to sell or refrain from selling. But in any case we have not reached the end of our task.

In the first place, in the case of most ordinary commodities, the proposition that value depends on conditions of demand and on quantity available is not the end of the story. We can take a further step and say that the quantity of them available depends in the long run on the ease or difficulty of producing them, and that their value has some tendency to equal, in some sense, their cost of production. The question now arises, can we take this further step with money? Are there any forces at work tending to make the quantity of money available dependent on the difficulty of producing it, and its value therefore equal to its cost of production? If not, by what other forces is a limit set to the quantity of money available?

Secondly, we have so far felt entitled to treat the demand for money and the quantity available as independent and disconnected things. But unfortunately the facts seem to show that if we are studying a process of continuous change, they are *not* wholly disconnected with one another. In other words, a continuing change in the quantity of money available may affect the conditions of demand for it, and vice versa. These complications become extremely important in examining the behaviour of thoroughly disorganised monetary systems, or in tracing the connection between money and the ups and downs of trade: but to preserve our sanity we are entitled to defer them till later in this book. We must, however, proceed at once to pick up the first of the loose threads just mentioned, and to enquire how the quantity of money in existence is determined. The answer to that question, unlike those with which we have been concerned hitherto, is not simple and universal, but depends upon the *kind* of money and money-system with which we are dealing. To a consideration, therefore, of the different kinds of money which exist we must now go forward.

CHAPTER III

THE QUANTITY OF MONEY

'What's the use of their having names,' the Gnat said, 'if
they won't answer to them?'

'No use to *them*,' said Alice; 'but it's useful to the people
that name them, I suppose. If not, why do things have names
at all?'

'I can't say,' said the Gnat.

Through the Looking-glass

1. The Kinds of Money

**§ 1. Bank Money and Common Money: Legal Tender, Optional
and Subsidiary Money.** The last chapter left us with an important riddle which we could not solve without knowing something more about the various kinds of money which exist.
Now there have been and still are in the world many different
kinds of money and money-systems; and to give an exhaustive
account of all of them would far surpass the limits of this book.
But if we take some familiar piece of money—say a five-pound
note—if we treat it like a botanical specimen and ask it various
questions, the answers to which may help to distinguish it from
other kinds of money, then we may be enabled to build up some
sort of rough classification of money. And we can then go on
to get an idea of the ways in which the money-systems of the
world are built up out of these different kinds of money.

The first question we shall ask our five-pound note is this:
'Will you be accepted without question by anybody to whom
I offer you in payment of a debt?' And our note will answer
without hesitation, 'Provided it is somebody within this
country, yes. That is where I score over that cheque which

you sent to your tailor this morning.   He will only accept it
because he knows—or thinks he knows—that you have a balance
at your bank on which to draw; and because he has himself
facilities for passing it into his own bank.   But if you were a
farmer, it would be little use your trying to pay your labourers
with cheques, for they probably would not know what to do
with them.   And when you go to Little Puddlecombe for your
holiday in the summer, I should be a little shy, if I were you,
about insisting at once on paying all the local tradesmen by
cheque, until they get to know you a bit; for they may not be
altogether favourably impressed.   You will do better to take
me and some of my brothers with you: everybody will take us
without question in payment of a debt, and be thankful to
get us.'

Our note then belongs to the order of *common money*, or
money which is universally acceptable within a given political
area, and not to the order of *bank money*, which requires
special knowledge, and the making of special arrangements on
the part of the recipient.

Our next question will be this: 'My dear sir, do not take
offence, or misunderstand me.   I do not doubt for a moment
that *in fact* everybody will accept you: but tell me this, are they
bound to accept you, or is it open to them to decline to do so?'
And our note will bridle a little as he replies, 'Of course they
are bound to accept me.   The law says that anywhere within
this island I and my brothers are full legal tender for the discharge of a debt up to any amount.   That is what I cannot
stand about those silver and copper coins which I am always
knocking up against.   They give themselves great airs as
though they were legal tender people too; and so they are up
to a point, but only up to a point.   When you offered your
tobacconist a shilling and a penny for that packet of cigarettes,
he had to accept them: but if you had offered him thirteen
pennies he would have been entitled to refuse them.   And if
you had sent him forty-one separate shillings in payment of that
bill of £2 1s. he would have had the right to refuse *them*.   But
things so seldom happen that way that the shillings and the

pennies presume on your forgetting all about it, and get terribly above themselves.

'When I was travelling with an officer in the Middle East some years ago, I met a very interesting lady called a Maria Theresa dollar. She said that she had been travelling in those parts for nearly two hundred years without any Government passport at all, but that everybody seemed pleased to see her, because she was made of such good silver, and looked so kind and homely.[1] She said she could not see any point in being legal tender: she had always got on very well without it, and she seemed to regard it rather as a mark of ill-breeding and of not being quite sure of oneself. I believe I have some cousins in America too—the notes of the Federal Reserve Banks—who go about without any help from the Government beyond the fact that it is always glad to get them in payment of taxes; and they seem to get on all right. But personally I believe in being legal tender. These are queer times, and people sometimes get funny ideas into their heads; and if anything *should* happen—well, I've got my orders, and that clears *me*, as we used to say in the Army.'

Our note, then, belongs to the sub-order *full legal tender money*, or, as we call it for short, *legal tender*—that is, money which is certified by law to be valid in final discharge of a debt for any amount from one fellow-citizen to another; and not to the sub-order *subsidiary money*, which is only so certified for debts up to a limited small amount, or to the sub-order *optional money*, which is not so certified at all.

§ **2. Convertible and Definitive Money.** Let us return to our interrogation. 'I quite understand now, sir, that my tobacconist would be bound to accept you from me, and that I was bound to accept you from my employer. But should I have been bound to accept you *whoever* offered you to me? I seem to have heard something—forgive me if I am wrong—about there being somebody who is *not* entitled to offer you in final discharge of an obligation, and who would be bound, if I took

[1] See J. M. Keynes, *Economic Journal*, 1914, p. 260.

you to him, to give me some other kind of money instead. Is it true, please, that you are thus "convertible," or are you, as one might say, the last word?' And here our note will show his first signs of embarrassment. 'Well,' he will say, 'I hardly know what to reply. In the old days if somebody took me to the Bank of England, the man behind the counter used to be obliged to give him five gold sovereigns instead of me. During the war and the muddle that followed, the law, I was told, remained the same. But during all that time nobody ever tried it on with me but once. He was a fellow who lived in a cellar down by the Thames, and he had a great fire burning all day, and lots of funny pots and pans and things: and he took me and some of my brothers to the Bank of England, and asked for golden sovereigns: and—but the end of that story is too sad to relate. Since 1925 the position has changed again. If you were to take us now to the Bank of England the Bank would be obliged, under certain conditions, to give you a lump of gold in exchange for us; but that gold would not be *money*—you would not be able to spend it readily in exchange for goods and services, as you can me. So on the whole I feel rather less convertible inside than I used to do. At the same time, I'm clearly not the last word, as my friend the sovereign is, or as the rupee was in India up till 1927, or as the notes of most European countries were in those dreadful days after the war.'

This answer may be a little embarrassing to us as well as to the note: for the truth is that, as so often happens, the facts of life have become rather out of touch with the language invented by the writers of textbooks. But we must bravely set down our note as *convertible legal tender*, or money which one ordinary citizen must accept as final payment from another, but in exchange for which some central institution is bound to give something else if requested; and not as *definitive money*, or money in which even such a central institution is entitled to make a final and ultimate discharge of its obligations, including the obligation to convert convertible money. It should be noted that convertible legal tender is not the only sort of convertible money: bank money, for instance, and some kinds of optional money, carry the right to exchange them, on application to the proper quarter, for something else.

§ 3. Token and Full-bodied Money.

One more question, and our catechism is ended. 'You are a very fine-looking fellow and I do not want to say anything disparaging; but are you not, perhaps, a little flimsy and anæmic? If you were to give up working as money, and take up some other profession, do you think you could earn a living? Would people think as much of you as they do? Would you, to put it baldly, fetch as much?' And here our note will get really angry at last. 'How stupid and old-fashioned you are!' he will reply. 'You are contrasting me, I suppose, with that sovereign you are keeping—oh yes, I have been in your cash-box, and I know—and which would still be useful, if the worst came to the worst for stopping teeth. No, of course I should be no good except as money: why should I be? I should be no more use at house decoration or dentistry or other honest work than—if you will pardon my saying so—you would yourself. And let me tell you this, it's not only we paper pieces of whom that's true. There is my friend the rupee, for instance: he looks very smart and solid, and takes a lot of people in; but if you took his lettering off him, his carcase would come tumbling down in value. For it isn't his flesh that gives him the value he has got, it's the writing on him.

'And let me tell you this, too, if a great many of those haughty gold coins were to lose their money job simultaneously, they wouldn't be worth as much as they flatter themselves they would, not by a long way. They think men run after them so because they're strong and handsome, and so it was, when men were savages. But the chief reason men run after them now is because they're *money*. If one of them gives up the money profession while the rest stick to it, he's worth what he was before, because he can always get a money job again. But if they all got the sack at once, goodness knows where they'd be: for this dentistry yarn has worn a bit thin—there aren't all that number of rickety teeth in the world.

'You'll be saying next that the cattle of the ancient Greeks and the tobacco of the Red Indians and the knives of the Chinese were better money than I am, because you could use them to eat or to smoke or to kill people with. You might as well say that Harry Lauder would make a better Prime Minister than Mr. Baldwin, because he could make a living by singing comic songs if he got turned out of office. I admit that as things are I don't have quite such a good time if I go abroad as the sovereigns used to do. Foreigners don't seem to like the look of me quite so much; but they are an ignorant set of folk, and I don't pay much attention to them. No, I'm not ashamed of being only token money: to be legal tender is quite good enough for me.'

Our note, then, belongs to the race of *token money*, or money whose value is materially greater than the value of the stuff of which it is composed, and not to the race of what we will call *full-bodied* money, whose value is not materially greater than that of its component stuff. This distinction cuts across the rest of our classification. All bank money and all subsidiary money is normally token money: but of optional money some (like the United States Federal Reserve notes) is token, and some (like the big silver coins which circulate in the East) is full-bodied. Most convertible legal tender is token money, such as the bank-notes of most important countries before the war and again at the present day: but the sovereign *in India* is full-bodied convertible legal tender, for the Government of India is obliged to give $13\frac{1}{3}$ rupees in exchange for it on demand. Of definitive money again some (like the sovereign) is full-bodied, while some (like the notes of most European countries after the war) is token. For some purposes it is convenient to group together convertible legal tender (such as the Bank of England note) and token optional money (such as the United States Federal Reserve note) under the label of 'convertible common money.'

These results may be tabulated for convenience of reference as follows:—

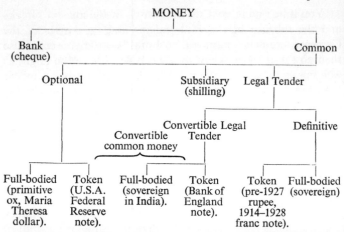

This classification, it will be observed, makes strange bedfellows. The rupee turns out to be only a silver note, or the 1914–1928 franc note a paper coin, whichever way we like to put it. The Maria Theresa dollar swallows her pride, and shares a stall with the primitive ox. Nevertheless this seems to be the classification which best satisfies the dictates of clear thinking.

II. The Quantity of Bank Money

§ **4. The Relation of Cheques to Deposits.** Modern monetary systems are built up by combining these different kinds of money in accordance with various rules of custom and law. It would be impossible, as the reader has already been warned, to discuss all these rules in detail within the limits of this little book: but by keeping steadfastly on the trail of our unsolved question, the question of how the quantity of money in a country is determined, we may learn a good deal about them. And we may legitimately simplify our task by excluding from our attention cases where money created abroad forms a conspicuous element in the money-system, as the Indian rupee, for instance, did until lately in East Africa, or the Maria

Theresa dollar does in the Arab world. With two of the kinds of money exhibited in our table, therefore, we shall not be bothered, namely full-bodied convertible legal tender (the sovereign in India), and full-bodied optional money (the Maria Theresa dollar).

The first question we shall ask is, how is the quantity of bank money in a country determined? To answer this, we must enquire rather closely how bank money is created. Now clearly cheques, which we have hitherto treated as synonymous with bank money, are not created directly by the banks: they are created directly by the people with cheque-books, who might appear to the uninitiated observer to draw cheques whenever they please for whatever sums they please—to create bank money at their own sweet will. But of course everybody knows really that this is not so, and that the cheque-book holder can only draw cheques up to a certain amount agreed upon between him and his banker, and that as a matter of fact he generally keeps well within this amount. This total amount up to which he has the right to draw cheques is sometimes called his 'deposit' at the bank; though it is perhaps as well to issue a warning that this is not quite the technical sense in which the banker uses the word. When a cheque for £10 passes from me to my butcher, and is paid in by him to the bank, my deposit at the bank is reduced by £10, and his is increased by the same amount: though £10 of money has changed hands, the total volume of deposits at the bank is unaffected. The relation between the total volume of deposits at any period and the total volume of cheques which passes during that period is thus a particular instance of the relation between the quantity of money *in existence* and the quantity of money *becoming available during a period* (p. 26). What we are now studying is the forces determining the size of a country's stock of money; and it is clearly the deposits themselves, and not the cheques drawn against them, which must be treated as forming part of that stock. A deposit which is not being drawn against is idling bank money, just as the shilling in my pocket is idling common money: and the passage of a cheque is a kind of transitory manifestation of bank money, as the passage of a bank note is a transitory manifestation of common money.

We may think of the deposit as a kind of generating station or mother-ship for cheques: and though it is a bad and foolish practice as a rule to create new names for common things, it may help us to bear this relation in mind, and also to avoid some cumbrousness of phrasing, if we call a person's deposit his *chequery*, because it is both a breeding-ground and a homing-place for cheques, as a rookery is for rooks. We shall speak then of an individual's chequery, but of a bank's deposits. The total of individual chequeries is the same thing as the total of bank deposits.

§ 5. The Relation of Deposits to Reserves of Common Money.

Bank money, then, is created not by the public but by the bankers, when they accord to the holders of cheque-books the right to draw cheques. Now the way in which bankers regulate the volume of their deposits, by varying the amount of the *loans* which they make to their customers, and the inner meaning of this whole business of banking, constitute a difficult and important subject which will require a whole chapter (Ch. V) to itself: but without pursuing it further at present we can quite well ask on what grounds the bankers arrive at their decisions about the total volume of deposits to be created. In Great Britain these decisions are left to the unfettered discretion of the bankers, that is, we may almost say, of those who control the policy of the five giant joint stock banks—Barclays, Lloyds, the Westminster, the Midland, and the National Provincial. But it is generally believed that the bankers regulate the volume of deposits in accordance with a customary rule of their own, which consists in keeping a certain rough proportion between their deposits and what are called their reserves: and as for the magnitude of this proportion, the figure of 9 to 1 is one which it is now convenient to keep in the head, though it would be wrong to speak as though it were either uniform for all banks or rigidly fixed for any individual bank. These reserves of the banks consist partly (at a guess, to the extent of two-thirds) of common money in their own possession, partly of a chequery at the Bank of England.   These chequeries are lumped with its other deposits by the Bank of England, which also appears to aim at keeping a certain rough proportion between its total deposits and its reserves, though it would be difficult nowadays to say what that proportion is supposed to be; before the war it was rather more than 2 to 1.   The fact that the Bank of England's proportion is thus flexible is of great importance in certain connections, and we shall have to return to it later: but for the purposes of our present broad survey, the fact that the Bank does not care to see its proportion vary beyond certain limits is the more important half of the truth.   The reserves of the Bank of England consist entirely of common money, namely, its own notes.   The chief point of this little extra complexity is that it facilitates the transfer of cheques between people who bank at different banks.   If A who banks at bank X pays a cheque for £10 to B who banks at bank Y, then bank Y, when it gets the cheque from B, will present it for payment to bank X: and bank X will meet its obligation by drawing a cheque for £10 on its chequery at the Bank of England.   As a matter of fact the stream of transactions of this nature between the big banks is so large and steady in all directions that the banks are enabled to cancel most of them out by means of an institution called the clearing-house: but the existence of these chequeries at the Bank of England facilitates the payment of any balance which it may not be possible at the moment to deal with in this way.

A thorough understanding of this process is important, for it will enable us to simplify several subsequent arguments by speaking as though there were only one bank in existence, leaving the reader to introduce for himself the complications required by the existence of several banks squaring up with one another by means of their chequeries at the Bank of England.   At the moment the important point is that the banks have got into the habit of treating these chequeries as part of their reserves.   The consequence is that the proportion between the total volume of the chequeries of the public and the total volume of real reserves of common money held by the banking system is appreciably larger than that proportion between his total deposits and total nominal 'reserves' which is the direct object of the individual banker's concern and calculations. But this does not affect the main upshot, which is that the volume of deposits is ultimately regulated with reference to the volume of the reserves of common money.

If we enquire why the volume of deposits should bear any reference to the volume of common money, the answer is not far to seek. It lies in the familiar fact that bank money is *convertible*. The right to draw a cheque carries with it the right to *cash* a cheque, that is to get it changed into common money by the bank which issues the cheque-book. Of course, if part of a chequery is thus removed in the form of common money, the size of the chequery is reduced by a corresponding amount. This right of conversion is used to a certain extent by all holders of cheque-books to obtain common money for making current payments of moderate amount: and it is used on a very large scale by 'capitalists' to obtain common money for the payment of wages. A bank therefore which gives the right to draw cheques must be able to lay its hands on enough common money to cash such proportion of those cheques as will in fact be presented for conversion. It is not surprising therefore that the banks should regulate their deposits with some reference to the amount of common money in their possession, or within their immediate reach.

§ 6. The Magnitude of Bank Reserves. If, however, we ask why the English banks have pitched upon this particular proportion of about 9 to 1, the answer is not so clear. Let us examine for a moment an imaginary banking system, which not only works securely (as ours does), but also works absolutely uniformly as between one day or week and another (as of course ours does not). There will then be no reason why such a banking system should keep any reserve of common money at all. For the common money which is paid out in exchange for cheques does not continue for ever in circulation: it finds its way back to the banks from the traders and shopkeepers to whom it is handed in payment for goods, and who thereupon dump it with the banks for safe-keeping, thus swelling their chequeries at the banks by a corresponding amount. No conceivable banking system could continue to exist which was always paying out common money and never getting it back again. But provided the inflow and outflow of common money were perfectly uniform, there would be no reason why there should ever be a standing pool of common money in the vaults of the banks. An instantaneous photograph of the banking system might well show us an enormous volume of deposits, and no reserves of common money whatever.

Now of course with any actual system the case is different. Both the needs of the cheque-book holders to draw common money, and the ability and willingness of the traders and so forth to dump common money, vary according to the day of the week and the season of the year. It would not be surprising, therefore, that an instantaneous photograph of our banking system at any moment should show a little pool of common money in the reservoir of the banks, sufficient to continue to feed the outgoing stream if the incoming stream should temporarily slacken. And it might be supposed that bankers would regulate the size of this pool according to the variations which experience leads them to expect in the suction which is drawing common money out and the pressure which is pumping it in. This, however, does not seem to be altogether the case. The pool is always considerably larger than would be necessary for that purpose, though its *average* level is quite certainly not so high as the uninitiated would gather from an inspection of the banks' monthly accounts.

Do the bankers then keep the pool large enough to meet any drain that could possibly be made upon it? Obviously they do not. If there were a very great increase in the suction of the cheque-book holders, or a very great slackening in the pumping zeal of the traders, the pool would not be sufficient. Nothing short of a proportion of 100 per cent between reserve of common money and deposits would suffice to meet all possible

eventualities. The practice of bankers is a compromise between keeping the pool which they expect in fact to be large
enough, and keeping the only pool which could possibly in all
circumstances be large enough. And it seems to be a compromise based rather on habit, and on the necessity of giving
depositors confidence in the strength of the bank, than on any
nice calculation of what events are reasonably likely and what
may be dismissed as 'unthinkable.'

It has been necessary to discuss this matter in some detail,
because it is one about which some confusion prevails—and
not only in the mind of the 'man in the street.' People sometimes tend to speak as though there was some mystic figure of
proportion or reserves to deposits—whether the English 1 to 9
or some other—without attaining which no banking system
can become respectable, and on attaining which any banking
system becomes unassailable. It is important therefore to
remember that in certain conditions a banking system could
work successfully without any reserve, and in other conditions
could only work successfully with a reserve of 100 per cent.

In continental countries the regulation of the volume of
bank money, which has not hitherto been of very great importance, is left as in England to the discretion of the banks:
but in the United States, where the predominance of bank
money in the money-system is as pronounced as in England,
the law has stepped in. Those banks (controlling about two-
thirds of the banking resources of the country) which are members of the nation-wide banking system are obliged to keep a
minimum proportion of reserves which works out at about
10 per cent on the average of 'demand' deposits, against which
cheques can be drawn without notice, and at 3 per cent of
'time' deposits, against which cheques can nominally only be
drawn if a month's notice has been given. The twelve Federal
Reserve Banks, which play in America something of the same
rôle as the Bank of England plays in England, are obliged to
keep, not indeed in common money but in coined or uncoined
gold, a reserve amounting to at least 35 per cent of their
deposits. A legal arrangement of this kind is open to the

objection that human nature being what it is, the law is sometimes held to encourage what it does not expressly forbid, and
a bank may therefore be tempted to keep its proportion of
reserves very near the bed-rock legal minimum. Any un-
expected demand for common money may then present the
bank with the alternative of infringing the law, or declaring
itself insolvent while its reserves are still far from exhausted.
For clearly if reserves are exactly 20 per cent of deposits, the
cashing of a cheque for a single dollar would reduce both
reserves and deposits by one dollar, and would therefore
reduce the proportion to under 20 per cent: and supposing that
to be the legal figure, the law would be broken. If a proportion fixed by custom is arbitrary and misleading, a proportion
fixed by law seems at first sight to be positively mischievous.
An iron ration which you must not touch even in the throes
of starvation is something of a mockery. Against such
criticism it may be urged (though not too loudly) that in finance
as in war rules are made to be broken on occasion, and that
their object is not to ensure that certain things shall never be
done, but that they shall not be done without good reason.
Certainly the American law does its best to guard against undue
rigidity. For in the first place the ordinary banks are obliged
to keep the whole of their *legal* reserves in the form of chequeries
with the Reserve Banks, so that since they cannot avoid keeping
also some common money as a first line of defence in their own
vaults, they cannot normally be lying right back on their
minimum legal proportion. Secondly, if their reserves are
running short, they are able, on conditions which will concern
us later, to replenish them by borrowing from the Reserve
Banks, which create chequeries in their favour just as a private
bank does for its customers. Furthermore, for reasons which
again will concern us later, the Reserve Banks themselves have
hitherto chosen to keep a much larger proportion of reserves
to deposits than the law compels: so that they can in practice
both expand their loans to the ordinary banks, and feed them
with common money, on a handsome scale without running any
risk of coming up against the law.

5

§ 7. **The Relation of Deposits to Common Money outside Bank Reserves.** Whether fixed by law or custom, the relation established in any country between the volume of bank money and the volume of common money kept *inside the banks* is seen to be somewhat arbitrary and artificial. It must not, however, be concluded that the relation which exists between the volume of bank money and the volume of common money circulating *outside the banks* is not, as things are, a natural and necessary one. Any banking system—including the imaginary one which we examined just now, and which had no *pool* of common money—would cease to work if at any time the *flow of* common money into the banks became very small as compared with the volume of deposits; and for this reason. There exists at any time a certain proportion, depending on the habits and customs of the people, between the volume of payments ordinarily made by cheque and the volume of payments ordinarily made in common money. The man with a cheque-book pays his butcher by cheque, but he pays strangers, or the booking-clerk at the railway station, in common money. This proportion is not of course fixed eternally: for instance, if the working-classes took to keeping banking accounts on a large scale and accepting payment of wages by cheque, the proportion of deposits to common money in circulation might become very much larger. The banks no doubt can exercise a gradual influence upon the habits of the community in this respect: but they cannot entirely control nor speedily change them. So long as these habits remain the same, and so long as the cheque-book holders have the right of demanding common money from their banks, the proportion between the volume of common money put into circulation and the volume of bank deposits will tend to remain unchanged. Any bank, therefore whose deposits greatly increased would find the outflowing stream of common money greatly exceeding the inflowing stream: for the public would be anxious to get hold of more common money to match the increase in bank money, and would be loth to part with what they had got. In such circumstances our imaginary banking system would break down like any other, indeed sooner than any other: for the assumption upon which it rests—the assumption of an equality between the inflowing and outflowing streams of common money—would be forthwith upset.

The relation between bank money and common money therefore depends only in part on the more or less arbitrary and conventional decisions of bankers regarding their reserves: it depends also partly on something more fundamental though not unalterable—the business habits and preferences of the community.

One more point. Our main preoccupation in this section has been the relation between bank money and common money. But so far as the law steps in, it takes no account of common money which is not legal tender, while it does sometimes take account of uncoined gold, which is not money at all. As regards actual practice, the pools and streams of common money consist partly of legal tender, partly of subsidiary money, and partly also (in some countries) of token optional money. But the quantity of subsidiary money is everywhere regulated by Governments, on the basis of their experience of the habits of their peoples, in some relation to the quantity of legal tender. And the quantity of token optional money (where such exists) is also, as we shall see in a moment, regulated with reference to the quantity of legal tender or of uncoined gold. What we have therefore in effect discovered is that the volume of bank money is regulated with reference to the volume of legal tender and of uncoined gold. How gold comes into the story we shall see in a few minutes.

III. The Quantity of Common Money

§ 8. The Relation of Convertible Common Money to Reserves. Our next task is to enquire how the quantity of convertible common money (the reader should refresh his memory of the definition on p. 39) is determined. The answer to this question varies somewhat according to whether the country in question does or does not possess any definitive money in active use. Before the war most Western countries made some use

of such definitive money in the shape of gold coins, and at the
present day the United States, Sweden, Norway, and some of
the British Dominions are still in the same position.　In these
circumstances, the proportion which convertible legal tender
bears to definitive money is influenced by the habits of the
people, in the same way as is the proportion which bank money
bears to common money in general.　There is no doubt that
the war has wrought a great change in popular habits in this
respect, so that even where gold coins are available, most people
do not show any great anxiety to obtain or use them.　In
England, as we have seen, Bank of England notes are not at
present convertible into gold coins; but most people seem to
agree that even if they were to become so there would be no
frantic rush to convert them.　The mere assurance of convertibility, it is thought, would have the same kind of soothing
effect as the sound of church bells in the distance, and be
equally unprovocative of action.

In all countries, however, there is a more obvious influence
limiting the volume of convertible common money, namely,
the voice of the law, which has intervened far more generally
in this matter than in the matter of bank money.　Sometimes
the law sets a limit to the total issue of some kind of convertible
legal tender, as was the case with the notes of the Bank of
France before the war, and is still the case with one of the many
kinds of American common money, the so-called 'Greenbacks'
or United States notes.　More usually it lays down rules about
the reserves which must be kept by Governments and banks
against the convertible common money which they permit to
circulate.　As to the character of these reserves more will be
said presently; for the moment let us simplify our task by
speaking as though they consisted entirely of definitive money.
As to the nature of the relation prescribed between the reserves
and the convertible common money, there have been two main
alternative practices.　The English practice, dating from the
celebrated Bank Act of 1844, has been to limit the 'uncovered'
or 'fiduciary' issue of convertible common money—the excess,
that is, of the total issue over the amount held of the stuff

prescribed as reserve.   Thus until 1928 the fiduciary issue of the Bank of England was limited by law to an amount which in that year had reached about £20 million; and from 1919 to 1928 the fiduciary issue of the Treasury Notes issued since 1914 by the Government was limited, not indeed by law but by Treasury ordinance, on the same lines.   In 1928 provision was made for amalgamating the two issues in the hands of the Bank of England, and the latter's fiduciary issue fixed afresh (though not unalterably) at £260 million.

Elsewhere than in England the alternative method of regulation, which consists in prescribing the minimum *proportion* of reserves to convertible common money outstanding, is almost universal.   Thus in America against two kinds of convertible legal tender (gold and silver certificates) a reserve of 100 per cent must be kept, against two kinds of token optional money (National Bank notes and Federal Reserve Bank notes) a reserve of 5 per cent, and against the remaining and most important kind (Federal Reserve notes) a reserve of 40 per cent.   In European countries, where the note-issue is for the most part now concentrated in the hands of central banks, similar provisions prevail.   Thus the Reichsbank has to keep a reserve of 40 per cent against its issues of notes, the Bank of France a reserve of 35 per cent, and the Russian State Bank a reserve of 25 per cent.

We cannot properly compare the merits of these two systems without having a clearer idea than we have yet had the opportunity to acquire about how we want the supply of money to behave.   But it is evident at once that the fixed fiduciary system is free from the defect which we noted, in connection with bank money, in the proportional system—namely, that it resembles the procedure of a certain municipality which tried to guard against a shortage of cabs by ordaining that there should always be at least one cab on the ranks.   The Bank of England, unlike the Reichsbank, would not come into conflict with the law till it had paid out the last penny of its reserves.   On the other hand, the proportional system makes it easier than does the fixed fiduciary system to expand the supply of convertible common money. If the Reichsbank receives an accession of one mark to its reserves it can expand its note-issue by $2\frac{1}{2}$ marks, whereas if the Bank of England receives an accession to £1 to its reserves it can only expand its note-issue by £1. As to whether this is on the whole a point in favour of the proportional system, we must suspend judgment.

§ 9. The Composition of Reserves. If it were true that the ultimate reserves held by the banking-system against bank money consisted entirely of legal tender, and that the reserves held against convertible common money consisted entirely of definitive money, we could now take a step forward by combining these results and laying down that the total quantity of money in a country is ultimately determined with reference to the quantity of definitive money which it possesses. For even though, as we have seen, the quantity of convertible common money has not quite always been regulated with direct reference to the reserves held against it, the fact that it is convertible has ensured in practice that a relation is maintained between the two. But in fact we are debarred from taking this attractive step. It is a small point that the reserves held against some kinds of token optional money (such as the American Federal Reserve[1] and national bank notes) may consist of convertible legal tender as distinct from definitive money, for the supply of convertible legal tender is itself subject to regulation.   But it is a material point that, as we have seen, the reserves held against bank money consist partly of uncoined gold; and it remains now to disclose that in many countries at the present day the reserves held against convertible common money also consist partly in uncoined gold and partly in something which seems at first sight to bear even less resemblance to definitive money—namely, in foreign securities and chequeries with foreign banks. We cannot get on therefore without looking more closely into this matter of the uncoined gold and the foreign securities and *émigré* chequeries. And that brings us face to face with two important topics known respectively as the gold standard and the foreign exchanges.

[1] The reserve held against these consists partly of Gold Certificates.

CHAPTER IV

THE GOLD STANDARD

'The cause of lightning,' Alice said very decidedly, for she felt quite sure about this, 'is the thunder—no, no!' she hastily corrected herself, 'I meant the other way.'

'It's too late to correct it,' said the Red Queen: 'When you've once said a thing, that fixes it, and you must take the consequences.'

Through the Looking-glass

§ **1. The Gold Bullion and Gold Circulation Systems.** In attempting to say what we mean by a gold standard, we are again met by the difficulty that the facts of life have escaped out of the pigeon-holes of the makers of text-books. But once more we must pluck up heart, and attach definite meaning to words rather than leave them shimmering in a haze. In this book, then, the phrase 'a gold standard' will be used to denote a state of affairs in which a country keeps the value of its monetary unit and the value of a defined weight of gold at an equality with one another. The reader is invited to pay particular attention to this definition, which as he will appreciate later is framed with a certain low cunning.

Since the value of money depends among other things on the quantity of it in existence, a policy of keeping this value at an equality with that of a defined weight of gold involves the regulation of the supply of money, and demands therefore from the central monetary authority (whether this be the Government or a Central Bank or a combination of the two) a certain measure of continuous and conscious activity. But provided the rules and practices about reserves which we examined in the last chapter are pretty rigidly adhered to by

53

the several parties concerned, there are various devices available for diminishing the element of conscious initiative, and increasing the element of automatic response, in the actions of the central authority. The most obvious of these devices is for the central authority to be put under obligation to be always prepared, on the one hand, to convert at least some one important kind of convertible money into uncoined gold at a fixed rate, and on the other hand to buy uncoined gold for money at a fixed rate. For in this case, if the value of money shows signs of rising above the value of the defined weight of gold, gold will be offered for sale to the monetary authority, which will thus be enabled, without altering its practice about reserves, to expand the supply of money, which will consequently fall in value. If on the other hand the value of money shows signs of falling below that of the defined weight of gold, people will bring money to the central authority for conversion into gold, and the central authority, if it is to maintain its practice about reserves unchanged, will be obliged thereupon to curtail the supply of money, thus bringing about a rise in its value. This is the system now in force in Great Britain, where the Bank of England is obliged to buy standard gold at the rate of £3 17s. 9d. an ounce, and to sell gold bars, of a minimum weight of about 440 ounces, in exchange for its notes at a price of £3 17s. 10½d. an ounce. This arrangement is known as the gold bullion system, and it is natural that where it prevails gold bullion, that is uncoined gold, should play a leading part in the rules about reserves.

In countries such as England before the war, which make use of a full-bodied definitive money made of gold, a slightly more elaborate procedure is adopted. The central authority is put under obligation to be always prepared, on the one hand, to convert at any rate some one important kind of convertible money into gold money, and on the other hand to turn gold into gold money at a charge which does no more than cover the bare cost of minting. Before the war the possession of a gold money was so widely and deeply felt to be essential to national respectability that it would have been pretty commonly maintained that a country which had not got an arrangement of this kind could not be said to have a gold standard. In the light of our idea of a standard, however, we see that this 'gold circulation system,' as we may call it, is simply one device among others for facilitating the maintenance of a gold standard.

It must be noted that in order to make the first limb of this system effective in conditions in which the value of money has fallen below that of the defined weight of gold, it must be permissible and practicable to turn the gold money obtained from the central authority into uncoined gold, or to export it for use in other countries. Otherwise its value will remain no greater than that of the other units of the money-supply, and there will therefore be no inducement to ask for it. Thus between 1914 and 1925, when various obstacles existed in the way of the melting and export of sovereigns, England was not on a gold standard. It must be noted further that unless the system (and the same applies to the gold bullion system) has both its limbs intact, the gold standard will not be unconditionally prescribed by law. Thus in Sweden, while notes are convertible into gold coin, the Bank of Sweden reserves the right to decline to buy unlimited gold at a fixed rate; and if it exercised this right in certain conditions, the value of Swedish money would come to exceed the value of the weight of gold mentioned in the law, and the gold standard would have ceased to exist.

§ 2. The Bimetallic and Limping Systems. It is of interest at this point, in the light of our knowledge of the meaning of a standard, to glance briefly—we can do no more—at certain monetary systems which have existed and attracted much attention in the past. In France from 1803 to 1870 there were two kinds of full-bodied definitive money, one made of silver and one of gold, and both these metals were freely accepted at the mints for coinage into money. This system was commonly described as the double or bimetallic standard: its purpose was to prevent the country suffering from a shortage of money owing to a failure in supply of one of the metals, and it was persuasively urged by many people that if the whole world would adopt similar arrangements the value of money could be kept much more stable than would otherwise be the case. Into these claims we cannot enter: our only business here is with the nature of the system and with its name. What happened in practice is that that metal only whose supply was for the time being rapidly expanding was brought to be coined, and came therefore to predominate in the money-supply, including the reserves which the monetary authority drew upon to convert its notes. Thus it so happened that for about fifty years the value of French money was being kept equal to that of a defined weight of silver and for the remainder of the period to that of a defined weight of gold. We see, therefore, that the phrase 'bimetallic standard' is a misnomer; France had throughout the period a bimetallic *system*, but she had first a silver and then a gold *standard*. And while throughout the period she had two kinds of definitive money, she had at any moment only one kind of money of which it could be said that the monetary authority was trying to keep the value of the franc equal to that of a defined weight of the metal of which that money was composed. Turning back therefore to our table on p. 40, we can make a new refinement, dividing definitive money into *standard money*, or money in which the central authority is *in fact* making its final payments, and *definitive non-standard money*, in which the authority is *entitled* to make its final payments, but is not in fact doing so. Even this refinement will let us down in certain transitional periods. Thus from about 1850 onwards gold was coming to predominate in the French money supply, and the value of the franc to conform to that of a defined weight of gold: but until 1860 the Bank of France managed to continue to make its final payments in silver. Whether the gold or the silver money was standard money during that period is a nice problem of terminology: but since such situations can only be transitory, it does not much matter how we solve it.

The same kind of considerations arise in connection with the monetary system which prevailed in France, and the other countries of the so-called Latin Union with which she joined for certain monetary purposes, from the 'seventies till the outbreak of the war. Though these countries had abolished the unlimited coinage of silver, they still possessed large quantities of silver coins, which had once been full-bodied but were now token money; and their central authorities reserved the right to make final payment in these coins instead of in gold coins when it suited their convenience to do so. This arrangement was generally described as a 'limping standard'—the idea being that the standard had as it were two legs, one of gold and one of silver, but that the silver leg was crippled and deformed. But we see now that while the arrangement can be reasonably described as a limping *system*, it was not a standard at all. During the greater part of the period in question the Bank of France kept the gold standard in operation: and when at intervals and for short periods it exercised its option of paying out in token silver money in such wise as to let the value of the franc fall below the value of the weight of gold defined in the law, we can only describe its action by saying that it set up for the time being an *arbitrary* standard, as many countries did later during the war. In the United States, the existence of a certain quantity of non-standard token definitive money of this kind (silver dollars) has not prevented the unbroken maintenance of a gold standard.

§ 3. Foreign Exchange under Arbitrary Standards.

So much for the coined and uncoined gold in the reserves: now what about the *émigré* chequeries? To understand these we have to plunge into a subject of which little has hitherto been said —the relation between the monetary systems of different countries, and to examine the forces which determine the level of the *foreign exchanges*—that is to say, the value in terms of one another of the moneys of two countries—let us call them England and Utopia—whose inhabitants are in business communication with one another. And first, how does it come about that either money has any value in terms of the other— that pounds are quoted at all in terms of utopes or vice versa?

The answer is that since the inhabitants of the two countries are in business communication, there will be some Englishmen who have claims to Utopian money and desire to dispose of them for English money, and other Englishmen who desire to obtain such claims in exchange for English money. The former class will include those who have sent goods to Utopia and sold them there, or have rendered other services to residents in Utopia, or are receiving interest payments on capital invested in Utopia in previous years. The latter class will include those who have ordered goods in Utopia for which they have to pay or have availed themselves in other ways of the services of Utopians, or find themselves obliged to remit interest on capital originally borrowed in Utopia, or desire to invest their savings in Utopia. There will of course be Utopians too who desire, for corresponding reasons, to dispose of or to obtain English money; but we can fairly simplify matters for ourselves by supposing for the moment that all the dealings (whether between Utopians or Englishmen) are in claims to Utopian money, and that they all take place in England, where these *claims* to Utopian money are bought and sold for *actual* English money.

Now we can turn to our main question—what determines the rate of exchange between pounds and utopes? It will be both simplest and most instructive to start with the case in which both England and Utopia are on arbitrary and independent standards, as so many countries were in the years immediately after the war. But we will assume, what in those years was by no means true, that both countries are in a state of comparative stability as regards their monetary affairs, so that we have not to deal at present with the complicating effects of violent and continuous monetary dislocation. And we will suppose further for the moment that there is only a mathematical line between the two countries, and that neither imposes import or export duties. Under these conditions, it has become customary to assert that the normal level of the rate of exchange depends on the relative price-levels, in the moneys of the two countries, of the things which enter into trade between them. Supposing for instance a quarter of wheat costs £5 in England and 25 utopes in Utopia, the rate of exchange will tend to settle at 4s. to the utope or 5 utopes to the £. The matter is ordinarily argued in this way. Suppose at any time a utope came to cost only 3s. instead of 4s., people would spend 75s. in buying 25 utopes, with these utopes buy a quarter of wheat in Utopia, sell the wheat for £5 in England, and thus make a profit of 25s. Suppose on the other hand a utope will sell for as much as 5s., then people would devote £5 to buying a quarter of wheat in England, sell the wheat for 25 utopes in Utopia, sell these utopes for 125s., and so again make a profit of 25s. And in either case so many people will engage in similar transactions as in the first case to force up, in the second case to drive down, the price of utopes till it reaches the old level of 4s. Thus our proposition seems to be established. It is usual to add that the rate of exchange may at any time diverge from its normal level within limits depending on the amount of the transport charges and duties (if any) on these goods most likely to be transported between the two countries. Suppose for instance the cost of transporting a quarter of wheat between Utopia and England is 25s. the price of utopes might sink as low as 3s., or rise as high as 5s., without leading to any movement of wheat, or therefore to any corrective movement of the exchange.

But if the reader happens to have any experience in international business, he will probably cry out that we have got into a muddle about the causal sequence of events, like Alice about the lightning and the thunder. For he will know that in real life if the price of Utopian money rises, the price of wheat in Liverpool at once rises to match, and he will conclude that it is the exchanges that determine the price of traded goods and not the other way round. And in the case of any individual transaction this may be true, particularly if, as in the case just considered, the traded article is an *import* of which the country in question is only one among many buyers. What perhaps our experienced trader does not see is that if these price-rises occur on any great scale, and if the supply of money in England is not altered in any way, Englishmen as a whole will not be able to buy so many goods as before; fewer Utopian goods will be imported into England, and more English goods exported to Utopia. There will thus be larger supplies of utopes in the hands of Englishmen, and a diminished pressure on the part of other Englishmen to obtain them; and the price of utopes will have to fall again. Thus, given the price-level of traded goods in terms of utopes, the fact that the maintenance of a certain price-level in terms of pounds is rendered possible by the monetary situation in England turns out to be the essential condition for the maintenance of a given rate of exchange. And in this puzzling universe to say that the maintenance of one thing is the essential condition for the maintenance of another is often just about all we can hope to mean by saying that the one thing is the cause of the other.

The proposition under debate, therefore—that the rate of exchange between two countries with arbitrary standards depends on the relative purchasing power of the moneys of the two countries over those goods which are the subject of trade between them—while it is sometimes argued in an unconvincing fashion, and while in any case it does not tell us the *whole* truth about the determination of the rates of exchange,[1] seems to the present writer to be sensible and helpful as far it goes. For knowing what we do about the connection between the value of money in any country and its supply, it serves to remind us that the exchange rates are also connected with the supply of money in the two countries. If for instance we were to find at a later period that the supply of Utopian money had become double what it was at the period of our first survey, while neither the supply of English money nor any of the other conditions of the problem had changed, we should not be surprised to learn that the rate of exchange had become 10 utopes to the pound instead of 5.

[1] Under independent standards, the rate of exchange between two countries depends also on the same forces as, under a gold standard, determine the relative levels of money wages and internal prices in the two countries. These forces are discussed on p. 126 and the reader is advised to defer consideration of this point till he reaches that page.

§ **4. Foreign Exchange under a Gold Standard.**   Let us next suppose that England and Utopia are each maintaining a gold standard, through the operation of a gold circulation or gold bullion
system.   Neglecting hindrances to transport, it will still be true
that the normal rate of exchange between them depends on the
relative values of their moneys in terms of traded goods.   But
since gold is among the goods which become most easily the
subject of trade, we can simplify matters by saying that the
normal rate of exchange depends on the relative values of the
two moneys in terms of gold, that is, on the relative weights of
gold defined in the laws of the two countries as the bases of their
respective standards.   And refining further, we can say that
the actual rate of exchange cannot diverge from this normal
level in either direction by an amount which exceeds the cost
of sending gold from one country to the other.   For if the
price of utopes rose beyond this point, it would pay Englishmen to buy gold for pounds, send it to Utopia, and sell it there
for utopes, rather than to buy claims to utopes on the exchange
market; and the swollen demand for utopes on the exchange
market would therefore subside.   And conversely with a movement in the other direction.   Thus with gold standards, unlike
arbitrary standards, the normal rate of exchange is both in-
variable and definitely calculable without the aid of those
precarious index-numbers of which we acquired in Chapter II
a certain distrust: and further the possible variations from this
normal rate are themselves capable of being predicted and
expressed in definite terms.

Historically indeed, it is this relative fixity of the exchanges
under a gold standard which has furnished the main incentive
to numerous countries to establish or to restore one; and it is
chiefly for the purpose of checking movements in the exchange
rates that monetary authorities are nowadays called upon to
draw on their reserves of gold.   This fact explains why the
Bank of England is only obliged to give gold for its notes in
minimum quantities of about £1700 worth; for smaller
quantities than that are hardly likely to be useful for purposes
of international remittance.   It also throws light on a curious

anomaly in the English monetary system. For in England, as has been explained, the kind of money which predominates in importance is bank money, and it is in fact bank money which the business world uses to buy gold from the Bank of England for export. One might have expected therefore that if the matter of gold reserves was to be regulated by law at all, it would have been regulated by establishing some direct connection between the gold reserve and the volume of that kind of money which is actually utilised on occasion for the purchase of gold. But in fact, as we have seen, the Bank of England's gold reserve is held directly against its notes, which are not convertible into gold coin, and which are not likely to be used by the public for conversion into uncoined gold for export. The system is a relic of a time when Bank of England notes were both the most important form of money and were also liable to be presented by the public in large quantities for conversion into sovereigns for internal use. These conditions having passed away, it is, to say the least of it, a confusing arrangement; and some people think it is a pity that advantage was not taken of the fusion of the Bank of England and Treasury note-issues in 1928 to change it altogether.

§ **5. The Gold Exchange System.** Now at last we are in sight of those *émigré* chequeries, whose scent drew us along this trail of the foreign exchanges. Suppose now that England has a gold circulation or gold bullion system, and that Utopia has not; but suppose that Utopia decides to establish a gold standard and wishes for some kind of artificial stiffener—a kind of corset or Dr. Scholl's metatarsal arch support—to strengthen her resolution and lighten her intellectual task in maintaining it. It may perhaps occur to her that since English money is being kept stable in terms of gold, she will have succeeded in maintaining a gold standard if she can keep stable her rate of exchange with England; and that the latter result will be ensured if her monetary authority is always prepared to sell claims to English money to Utopians, and to buy claims to English money from them, at a fixed rate. But of course in order to be sure of doing this, the Utopian monetary authority will have to keep a stock of claims to English money; and it is quite natural therefore that in the Utopian reserve regulations chequeries with English banks, and English securities which can readily be sold in exchange for such chequeries, should play the same leading part that is played in the English reserve regulations by coined or uncoined gold.

This sytem, which is known as the gold exchange system, was invented before the war independently by certain European countries such as Austria which wished to economise in the use of gold, and by the Government of India. The history of its development in India, which was gradual and almost acci-dental, is of particular interest. It so happens that India tends normally to export goods of greater aggregate value than she imports, so that there were normally plenty of exporting mer-chants who possessed English money and were anxious to obtain money in India. The Government on the other hand was normally in the position of holding money, derived from taxation, in India, and of wishing to obtain money, with which to pay interest charges, pensions, and so forth, in London. Thus the two parties had come together naturally on the exchange market, before there was any thought of using that market deliberately for the regulation of the money supply. Further, owing to this same piling-up of English money in the hands of exporters from India, the normal tendency was for the value of the rupee to rise in terms of pounds rather than to fall. Hence even when regulation was fully developed, it was as a rule sufficient for the Indian Government to announce its willingness to sell, in London, claims, known as Council Bills, to rupees in India, in unlimited amounts at or near the fixed rate of 1s. 4d. a rupee. It was only occasionally that owing to famine in India or for other reasons the 'balance of trade' turned the other way; and then the Government stepped in to prevent the value of the rupee in terms of pounds from falling, by selling for rupees in India a certain number of claims to pounds in London, known as Reverse Council Bills. During the war and the ensuing confusion the system broke down

6

completely; but it was gradually restored after 1924, though it was not till 1927 that the Government was for the first time placed under legal obligation to convert rupees into gold exchange in unlimited amounts at any time—at the rate now of a little less than 1s. 6d. a rupee. It is for this reason that in our table on p. 40 the pre-war rupee is described as definitive and not as convertible money.

The gold exchange system has been widely adopted in the monetary legislation of countries with a dependent political status—such as West Africa, Palestine and the Philippines— which is perhaps one reason for its unpopularity with Indian political opinion. But since the war it has also been adopted in its essentials by a number of countries—such as Russia, Germany, and Italy—whose sovereign status nobody would question, but which desired to re-establish a gold standard without indulging in the luxury of keeping a big stock of gold. For while of course reserves of gold exchange have to be obtained, no less than gold, out of the proceeds of saving or borrowing, they can earn a little interest even while functioning as reserves. Further they can easily and speedily be released for investment in more lucrative securities, and again built up again out of the proceeds of the sale of such securities, in accordance with the changing needs of the situation; whereas the trundling of gold to and from market is a relatively cumbrous and expensive proceeding. Thus the gold exchange system is a convenient one for impecunious countries, as well as profitable though sometimes rather embarrassing for the countries selected as custodians of reserves. Indeed, so convenient is it that even a country like France, which has established a full gold bullion system by law, may continue to operate the gold standard largely by means of dealings in foreign exchange. On the other hand, so strong is the sentiment still attaching to the possession of actual gold that even those countries which have adopted the gold exchange system have tended to accumulate a stock of gold as well, and to preserve the option of converting their notes into actual gold. Further only in some cases have definite rules about convertibility been put into force at all: in other cases, while the monetary authority preserves stability of the exchanges in practice by means of its dealings in exchange, the only legal provisions in force are those prescribing the size and composition of the reserves.   The objection to giving a list of these two classes of countries is that it might be out of date by the time it reached the reader's hands; and in any case from the practical, as opposed to the formal, point of view the distinction is not of much importance.

§ 6. **The Value of Money and the Value of Gold.**   We can now resume the main thread of our argument.   In a gold standard country, whatever the exact device in force for facilitating the maintenance of the standard, the quantity of money is such that its value and that of a defined weight of gold are kept at an equality with one another.   It looks therefore as if we could confidently take a step forward, and say that in such a country the quantity of money depends on the world value of gold. Before the war this would have been a true enough statement, and it may come to be true again in the lifetime of those now living: it is worth while therefore to consider what, if it be true, are its implications.

   The value of gold in its turn depends on the world's demand for it for all purposes, and on the quantity of it in existence in the world.   Gold is demanded not only for use as money and in reserves, but for industrial and decorative purposes, and to be hoarded by the nations of the East: and the fact that it can be absorbed into or ejected from these alternative uses sets a limit to the possible changes in its value which may arise from a change in the demand for it for monetary uses, or from a change in its supply.   But from the point of view of any single country, the most important alternative use for gold is its use as money or reserves in other countries; and this becomes on occasion a very important matter, for it means that a gold standard country is liable to be at the mercy of any change in fashion not merely in the methods of decoration or dentistry of its neighbours, but in their methods of paying their bills.

For instance, the determination of Germany to acquire a standard money of gold in the 'seventies materially restricted the increase of the quantity of money in England.

But alas for the best made pigeon-holes! If we assert that at the present day the quantity of money in every gold standard country, and therefore its value, depends on the world value of gold, we shall be in grave danger of falling once more into Alice's trouble about the thunder and the lightning. For the world's demand for gold includes the demand of the particular country which we are considering; and if that country be very large and rich and powerful, the value of gold is not something which she must take as given and settled by forces outside her control, but something which up to a point at least she can affect at will. It is open to such a country to maintain what is in effect an arbitrary standard, and to make the value of gold conform to the value of her money instead of making the value of her money conform to the value of gold. And this she can do while still preserving intact the full trappings of a gold circulation or gold bullion system. For as we have hinted, even where such a system exists it does not by itself constitute an infallible and automatic machine for the preservation of a gold standard. In lesser countries it is still necessary for the monetary authority, by refraining from abuse of the elements of 'play' still left in the monetary system, to make the supply of money conform to the gold position: in such a country as we are now considering it is open to the monetary authority, by making full use of these same elements of 'play,' to make the supply of money dance to its own sweet pipings.

Now for a number of years, for reasons connected partly with the war and partly with its own inherent strength, the United States has been in such a position as has just been described. More than one-third of the world's monetary gold is still concentrated in her shores; and she possesses two big elements of 'play' in her system—the power of varying considerably in practice the proportion of gold reserves which the Federal Reserve Banks hold against their notes and deposits (p. 47), and the power of substituting for one another two kinds of common money, against one of which the law requires a gold reserve of 100 per cent and against the other only one of 40 per cent (p. 51). Exactly what her monetary aim has been and how far she has attained it, is a difficult question of which more later. At present it is enough for us that she has been deliberately trying to treat gold as a servant and not as a master.

It was for this reason, and for fear that the Red Queen might catch us out, that the definition of a gold standard in the first section of this chapter had to be so carefully framed. For it would be misleading to say that in America the value of money is being kept equal to the value of a defined weight of gold: but it is true even there that the value of money and the value of a defined weight of gold are being kept equal to one another. We are not therefore forced into the inconveniently paradoxical statement that America is not on a gold standard. Nevertheless it is arguable that a truer impression of the state of the world's monetary affairs would be given by saying that America is on an arbitrary standard, while the rest of the world has climbed back painfully on to a dollar standard.

§ 7. The Value of Gold and its Cost of Production. The last section contained nothing to interfere either with our proposition that in a gold standard country the value of money is equal to that of a defined weight of gold, or with our proposition that the value of gold depends on the demand for it and the quantity of it in existence. All that it did was to point out a highly peculiar future in the present demand for gold. There is nothing therefore to prevent us from asking the question which, if we have any knowledge of the general theory of value, we shall naturally be impelled to ask—namely, whether we can take the further step of saying that the quantity of gold in the world depends on its cost of production, and that its value tends to equal its cost of production. Half a century or so ago it would have been very difficult to assert anything of the sort; for the discovery of gold was in those days something of a windfall, and its production was not carried on with any close

regard to costs. The great gold discoveries of the 'fifties in
Australia and California were largely fortuitous, and production, for those who were successful, was mainly a matter of
washing free of sand the gold in surface deposits, and bringing
it to market. But there has been a considerable change in this
respect in recent years, for the surface deposits of gold are
practically exhausted, and what may be called picture-palace
methods of production are obsolete. Gold mining, especially
in the Transvaal, is now a matter of costly chemical and
mechanical processes, and conducted like any other business
with a careful eye to receipts and costs. Any great change in
the value of gold therefore speedily influences the actions of
gold producers. The means by which it affects them depends
on whether they live in a gold standard or a non-gold standard
country. In the former case there is a change in their money
expenses of production, in the latter a change in the money
price which they get for their product: in either event there is
likely to be an appreciable effect on their annual output of gold.
For if the value of gold falls they will curtail their production,
and if it rises they will expand their production, just as would
the producers of any other commodity in like case. Thus
there is a tendency with gold, as with other things, for its value
to correspond with what we will call its marginal cost of production—that is, with the cost of production of that part of the
annual output which is wrested with most difficulty from the
lap of Nature.

We must not, however, conclude from this that there is any
tendency for the value of gold to remain *stable*. For the marginal cost of production of gold, like that of most other things,
is not a fixed amount, but varies according to the quantity
produced. Thus a great fall in the value of gold, due to a
falling off in the world's demand, would lead to the closing
down of a number of the more unfertile mines (or parts of
mines) which it no longer paid to work; and the new marginal
costs, being those of more easily won gold, would be in
harmony with the reduced value of gold. But this restriction
of output would not be likely to have much effect in causing

the value of gold to rise again. For first, the whole annual output of gold is only a small proportion—about 2 per cent—of the world's total supply, so that even a large percentage decrease in the annual output would only lead to a less rapid increase, and not to a decrease, in the total supply. Secondly, if the proportion of output which comes from the so-called 'low-grade' or infertile mines and parts of mines is not great, a fairly small reduction in output will suffice to bring the marginal costs of production into correspondence with the reduced value of gold. As a matter of fact the fall of about 50 per cent in the value of gold between 1915 and 1919 was accompanied by a decrease of only about 22 per cent in the annual output, and of course by an actual increase in the world's total stock. And somewhat similar reasoning suggests that a great rise in the value of gold would not be likely of itself to lead to a great proportionate increase in the world's stock.

We can say, then, that the quantity of gold in existence is ultimately limited by the cost of production of gold, but not that it depends on it in any direct and simple manner. And we can say that the value of gold tends to equal its marginal cost of production, but not (if we fear the anger of the Red Queen) that it is determined by it. Further, we must remember that these facts do not imply that the value of gold tends to remain stable. Bearing all this in mind we may fairly say that in a gold-standard country the quantity of money will be ultimately limited, if by nothing else, then by the cost of production of gold, and that in any case its value tends to equal the marginal cost of production of a given weight of gold.

CHAPTER V

MONEY AND SAVING

'And the moral of that is—"The more there is of mine, the less there is of yours."'

Alice's Adventures in Wonderland

§ 1. A Preliminary View of Bank Loans. In the last three chapters we have examined in broad outline the more persistent of the forces which are operating in any country to make the value of money what it is. But before we are ready to debate high matters of monetary policy, we have still certain tasks to perform. And the first of these is to develop the hint dropped on page 42 that the quantity of bank money depends on the *loan* operations of the banks, and to see if we can dispel some of the fog which in the minds of many people, including not a few eminent bankers, clings about this whole business of banking.

Let us begin by looking at a perfectly ordinary transaction. An apple farmer, let us say, who expects to harvest his crop in six months' time, applies to the bank for a loan of £1000; and the bank creates for him a chequery of £1000, thus giving him the right to draw cheques, or to withdraw common money, up to that amount, as and when he requires. Within these limits the farmer makes payments for the hire of labour, the purchase of materials, and his own personal expenses. At the end of the six months he gathers and sells his fruit, and repays his loan to the bank. Meanwhile the bank charges him interest upon it.

To the experienced business man there may seem nothing odd about the whole proceeding. But the reader without

practical experience of similar transactions need not be
ashamed to confess to a feeling of slight bewilderment. For
what has happened? By a wave, apparently, of the bank's
magic wand the farmer and his men have been enabled to live
for six months at the expense of the rest of the community:
the bank has given them a claim on the community's real
income of food and clothing and tools and cinema shows.
And for rendering this service to the farmer the bank charges
him something which it calls 'interest.' Our first impulse
surely is to cry out on the whole proceeding as a piece of
fraudulent legerdemain.

To see whether this attitude is necessarily just, let us frame
for ourselves a *possible* explanation—note that no more is
claimed for it at present than this—of what has really been
happening. In order to define the conditions of our problem,
let us assume for a start that the country with which we are
concerned is stationary in regard to population and technical
efficiency. And to simplify matters further, let us suppose
that there is only one bank (p. 43), and that its money is the
only kind of money in the country, everybody preferring to
make even the smallest payments by cheque; but that nevertheless it holds itself bound, as real banks do, by rules or
customs regulating the proportion of its reserves to its deposits.
These simplifications will much lighten our argument: when
they give rise to any special difficulty, it will be noted.

Our farmer must be regarded as making his purchases—
partly directly and partly through the medium of his workmen—from all kinds of producers and traders, whom we may
lump together under the title of 'the public.' The members
of the public pay the money so received into the bank, and
are thus enabled to build up a nest of chequeries at the bank.
When all the farmer's purchases have been made, his chequery
has vanished, and the public's new chequeries amount to
£1000. These chequeries, while their existence is a *consequence*
of the existence of the farmer's chequery, are quite different
from it in nature: for they have not been created by way of
loan, but have been built up out of the proceeds of rewards

for services rendered.   It seems to be clearly *possible* that they
represent a new and spontaneous act of saving on the part of
the public, which in building them up has refrained from
exercising its legal right to consume certain goods and services,
and has in effect transferred that right, through the agency of
the bank, to the farmer and his men.   And accepting this
explanation we see that as a result of this act of saving a new
piece of real wealth has, by the end of the six months, been
brought into existence—the apples have ripened on the trees.

§ **2. The Continuity of Bank Loans.**   Now let us try to carry
the story a little further.   The farmer receives a cheque for
£1000 in return for his crop, and pays it into the bank in
repayment of his loan.   This operation reduces the chequery
of the purchaser of the crop, and also the bank's total deposits,
by £1000.   Now we know that the bank aims at keeping a
certain proportion between its reserves and its deposits, and
there has been nothing in what has happened to alter either
its views about what this proportion should be or the actual
magnitude of its reserves (the reader will easily be able to
convince himself that this is still true even if we take account
of the existence of common money).   There is nothing therefore to deter it from increasing its deposits to their old figure
by making another loan of £1000, if it sees any point in doing
so.   And undoubtedly it will see great point; for on such a
loan it will get interest.   It will hold itself in readiness therefore
to make a new loan of £1000.

But to whom, the reader will be asking, has the farmer sold
his crop?   We shall keep nearest to real life by supposing
that he has sold it to a merchant; and we can keep quite near
enough to real life, and avoid unedifying complications, by
supposing that that merchant is a retailer, who proceeds to
unload the apples gradually on to the public in the course of
the next six months.   How does the merchant pay for the
crop?   Experience suggests that he borrows from the bank:
and since he is ready to borrow only a few minutes before the
bank is ready to lend, imagination suggests that somehow or

other this little mechanical difficulty about the time-interval will be got over, and that the £1000 which the merchant borrows *is* in effect the £1000 which the farmer repays. The rest of the public are unaffected by the transfer, and remain in possession of the chequeries which they have built up. We reach therefore the important conclusion that for the making of this second loan no *new* saving is required from the public.

But that, the reader will reply, is only natural; for we have supposed the whole of the merchant's outlay to consist in the purchase of the crop, neglecting such items as his shop rent and his personal expenses: and while, in the case of a merchant, this may be a legitimate simplification of the facts, it *ipso facto* precludes us from supposing that the public is called upon to undergo any new privation for the merchant's benefit during the currency of the second loan. Let us therefore carry the story a little further. As the merchant sells his apples, at the rate of say £40 worth a week, he will be in a position to pay back his loan bit by bit to the bank, and the bank will be in a position to make new loans to tailors, bootmakers—no matter whom, keeping always the aggregate of its outstanding loans at the constant level of £1000. And the public will not be called upon to undergo any new privation as the result of this state of affairs; for while it has to share its real income with the tailors and bootmakers who have been put in funds by the bank, that real income has been enhanced by the flow of apples out of the merchant's shop.

Thus our conclusion turns out to be perfectly correct—namely, that it is not necessary that every time the bank makes a loan a new act of saving should be performed by the public, or that in default of performing it they should be the victims of a fraud. And we shall be led to re-examine the story of our first loan as well, for of course it was only 'the first' in the sense that we chose to break at this particular point into the unending round of economic life, and not in the sense that we were trying to go back to the first syllable of recorded time. We shall have to consider the possibility that it was itself the successor of a previous loan which had been so used as to provide a flow of real income for the public, and that it therefore did not, as we supposed, demand any new act of saving on their part.

This conception of the continuity of loans is at first, perhaps, a little difficult to grasp. For some productive acts, such as the harvesting of a crop, are spasmodic, and it is natural that those who have just performed them should seize the opportunity of getting out of debt to the bank. But regarded as a whole, including the activities of manufacturing, marketing, and storage, the preparation even of foodstuffs for the consumer's use is a process almost as continuous as are the needs of the consumer; and the same is even more obviously true of the preparation of things such as tables or pots and pans, whose raw material is won from Nature by a process which is not subject to markedly seasonal variation. And while it may be rather unusual in normal times (though there is not much information available about this in England) for an individual firm to be continuously in the debt of its bank, there is no doubt that industry and commerce as a whole are continuously in the debt of the banks. In a stationary society, the carriage of such a continuous debt of constant amount, even though the individual recipients of loans were constantly varying, would require only that a single act of new saving should have been performed in the dim and distant past by the depositors of the bank. Under such conditions, the making of a bank loan is seen as the act not, as we were at first inclined to suspect, of a fraudulent magician, but of a faithful steward, administering to the best of its ability a fund of congealed saving which has been built up in the past.

§ 3. The Imposition of Forced Saving. So long then as the bank is only making new loans as old ones are repaid, all seems to be well. But now let us suppose that our new loan really was 'the first' in the sense that it constituted a net addition to the outstanding loans of the bank. Clearly this is not an impossible supposition: for there will always be so many people with unbounded confidence in their own abilities and good luck as to exercise a continuous pressure on the bank to expand its loans, and the bank itself, since it makes a profit on its loans, will be anxious to expand them as much as ever it dares. Supposing therefore it receives somehow (we need not for the moment enquire how) an accession to its reserves, we can be pretty sure that it will expand its loans by an amount several times as great as the increase in its reserves. Let us suppose now not only that our country is stationary, in the sense that it is not changing in respect of population or technical efficiency, but also that the disposition of the people as regards saving remains unchanged. In this case our original suspicions will be perfectly justified: the saving that is done to maintain the farmer and his men while the fruit is ripening will be done not voluntarily but perforce. And the way this forced saving is imposed on the public is through a fall in the value of money. The new money in the hands of the farmer and his men will stream on to the markets in competition with the money already in the hands of the general public. For a time shopkeepers may be able to meet the increased pressure to buy by drawing on stocks of goods; but before long at any rate they will put up the prices of their wares in order to make the limited stream of goods go round among their customers. Thus through the rise in prices the public is forced to share with the farmer and his men the real income which it would otherwise have had to itself.

It is true that the new money passes gradually into the possession of the public, and by the time the proceeds of the loan are all spent is entirely in their hands. But under the conditions we are now considering, this building up of chequeries represents no new real spontaneous saving on their part; it represents at best an attempt to prevent the real aggregate value of their money holdings from being permanently diminished by the fall in the value of the monetary unit. The 'saving' which they do is done under duress; and unlike ordinary saving it gives rise to no new fund of value in their possession which they can draw upon if they feel inclined to be extravagant at some future date.

In order to get our minds quite clear, let us examine the
situation at the end of such a period of forced saving, when
everything has settled down again.   The volume of bank loans
has permanently increased by, let us say, 10 per cent, and so
has the volume of money in the hands of the public.   But
since prices have risen 10 per cent, the aggregate real value of
the public's money supply is no greater than it was before.
Exhibiting their balance sheets, the bankers will point out
with pride that they balance—that every loan or other lucrative
asset is balanced by a liability to a depositor; and they will
plead that they are incapable of doing any harm to the public,
because obviously 'they can only lend what the public has
entrusted to them.'   Perhaps those of us who remember the
years 1914 to 1919 have always had our doubts about this; if
we have understood the preceding pages, we shall be able,
next time we hear it repeated in one of those admirable annual
speeches, to prove that it is not true.   And we shall find a
doubt growing up in our minds whether a banking system
which is tied by fixed rules about its reserves is likely to function
under all conditions to the public advantage.

Before passing on it is only fair to warn the reader that in
making the corrections necessary to adapt the argument of
this section to a multiple banking system, he may encounter
some little difficulty.   For with such a system, as every banker
knows, it is not open to a bank which receives an accession of
£1000 to its reserve immediately to expand its loans by eight
or nine times that amount.   And the reason is that it must be
prepared for its new creditors to draw a large proportion of
their cheques in favour of people who bank at other banks, so
that part of its new reserve will be drawn away (in England,
in the form of cheques on the Bank of England) to other banks.
The fewer the other banks, the larger its new loans will be;
but they may not, in the first instance, be much larger than the
new reserve itself.[1]   As the new reserve, however, gets distributed among the other banks, it will be possible for each

[1] See C. A. Phillips, *Bank Credit*, Ch. III: W. F. Crick, 'The Genesis
of Bank Deposits,' in *Economica*, June 1927.

of them to increase its loans by a moderate amount; and so, by a process of trial and error, the matter goes on until each bank has once more the proportion of deposits to reserve which it considers reasonable. And if there is some common force at work increasing the reserves of *all* the banks simultaneously, the process of adaptation will be very swift; for each bank will from the start be gaining from the other banks about as much as it is losing to them. Thus for exhibiting the broad result of an increase of reserves, our simplification turns out to be quite legitimate. But the point is of some importance psychologically, for it probably helps to explain the reluctance of many bankers to admit the decisive influence which their loan-policy exercises on the value of money.

§ **4. The Conversion of Spontaneous Saving.** Does it then follow that a virtuous bank must never make a net addition to the amount of its loans? By no means; there will be circumstances in which, if it omits to do so, it will be failing in its duty of acting as an intermediary for putting the genuine savings of the public at the disposal of industry and commerce.

Let us suppose that in a country which is still to be assumed stationary in respect of population and technical efficiency, the public, whether through a sudden wave of thrift or a sudden wave of distrust of more lucrative kinds of investment, desires to increase the amount of saving which it does through the mediation of the bank. How is this desire to show itself, and how is it to be utilised for the benefit of industry and trade? It is tempting to suggest that in real life people will do something which is ruled out by one of our simplifying devices— that they will carry common money into the banks and that the banks will lend it out to business men; and such a statement might fairly well represent what would happen under a primitive banking system. But it does not even approximately represent what happens in an Anglo-Saxon country to-day. In such a country nobody, broadly speaking, except shopkeepers, railway booking-clerks, and similar repositories of petty cash, can put anything into the banking system which

was not there already; and our convenient simplification does
no great violence to the facts. If the owner of a chequery at
the bank decides not to draw upon it for the purchase of a
new suit of clothes or a piece of house property, the bank's
total deposits (remember our other simplification of the single
bank) are not increased by a single penny beyond either what
they were to start with or what they would have been if the
depositor had decided differently. All that has happened is
that they have come to circulate rather more slowly. And
this statement gives us the key to the situation. For as the
daily stream of money coming on to the markets is reduced,
owing to the reluctance of depositors to spend their chequeries,
the owners of goods will find that in order to dispose of their
wares they will have to lower their prices—the value of money
will rise. Thus while the chequeries of the public have not
increased in money amount, they *have* increased in real value,
and the depositors have achieved their object of keeping a
larger store of real value in the form of money. But—and
this is the startling fact—they have achieved this object without
any of the usual inconveniences of saving—without being
obliged to refrain from the consumption of any desirable
goods and services. For, as explained above, the producers
and traders have reduced prices so as to get rid of the same
flow of goods and services as before.[1] The intended thrift of
the public has all gone to waste, and failed to benefit trade and
industry in any way.

Now suppose in these circumstances the bank adds to its
loans in such wise that the increased demand of those to whom
the new loans are made just balances the reduced demand of
the thrift-smitten depositors, and so prevents the shopkeepers
from lowering prices. If it acts in this way the bank will be
acting not as an oppressor but as a benefactor; it will not be
imposing unsought burdens on the public, but merely enabling
their thrifty intentions to bear fruit. In this event the new
money, as it is built up into the chequeries of the public, will

[1] Disregarding for the present any secondary effects of the falling
price-level in checking the creation of wealth (Ch. I, § 7).

faithfully represent the increased saving which they are doing. It is in fact such a process as this that we supposed to be happening in our original interpretation (§ 1) of the story of the loan to the apple farmer.

Now can we rely upon our actual banking system to behave in this way? Well, that depends to a certain extent on the exact rules and conventions in force. In America, as has been said (p. 46), the law prescribes a lower proportion of reserves against 'time deposits,' which cannot be drawn upon without notice, than against 'demand deposits,' which can. Now the increased thrift of depositors is likely to manifest itself to a certain extent in the conversion of demand deposits into time deposits, and so to enable the banks to expand their loans without infringing the law regulating their reserves. Such an expansion of time deposits at the expense of demand deposits has in fact been a very prominent feature of American banking history in the last few years. In England on the other hand the banks do not distinguish in their public accounts between 'deposit accounts,' which cannot be drawn upon without notice, and 'current accounts,' which can; and so far as is known they do not distinguish between them in framing their reserve policy, but keep about the same proportion of reserves to deposits in the broad sense, whether (as is usually the case in England, though not in Scotland) the deposit accounts are perceptibly less in volume than the current, or whether (as apparently sometimes happens) they are nearly as large.[1]   Thus we see a new reason for suspecting that a banking system which is tied by fixed rules about its reserves may not be well adapted to act under all conditions to the public advantage.

The reader will easily be able to work out the converse of the case just described. He will see that if the public decides to withdraw some of the real saving which they have done through the medium of the bank, and to that end begin to spend their chequeries faster, they will put up prices against one another, and so deprive one another of the increased

[1] Leaf, *Banking*, p. 124.

consumption which they had hoped to enjoy. Unless the
bank takes appropriate action by *reducing* the volume of its
loans, it will be imposing forced saving upon them no less
truly than if, in the absence of any such changed behaviour on
their part, it were to increase the volume of its loans as described in § 3. We cannot therefore finally assert, as we
asserted provisionally at the beginning of § 3, that so long as
the bank only makes new loans as old ones are repaid, all will
be well—if the bank so acts in the circumstances now under
consideration all will be far from well. And once more we
may well be doubtful whether what we have called the appropriate action in these circumstances can be expected from a
bank which is tied by fixed rules about its reserves.

§ **5. Bank Loans and Industrial Progress.** So far we have
legitimately simplified our task by assuming that the country
with which we are dealing is stationary in respect of population and technical efficiency. But, of course, most countries
in which we are interested are increasing year by year in
population and aggregate wealth, if not always in wealth per
head. It seems natural to suppose that if the bankers increase
their loans and therefore the money-supply year by year in
proportion to this increase in aggregate wealth they will be
doing no wrong: but after what we have learnt we may feel
inclined to be sceptical even about this. And we shall do well
to be sceptical, as the sequel will show: but if we suppose for
the present that the increase in aggregate wealth is entirely due
to the increase in population, and further that it proceeds year
by year at a uniform rate, we shall find, what it is always a
comfort to find, that the common-sense view is perfectly
correct. We may put the matter in this way. With a growing
population there is every year a new batch of persons who are
beginning to receive incomes (if only in the shape of pocket-
money) and to desire to perform saving in monetary form: and
unless the money-supply is expanded to match, we shall get
a situation somewhat resembling that depicted at the beginning
of § 4. For while these persons will no doubt succeed in

building up stores of money, their savings will be dissipated in the form of lower prices and increased consumption by the community as a whole, and will not be effectively put at the disposal of industry and trade.   Thus so far as an increase in bank money between any two dates is balanced by an increase in population, the bankers can sleep with easy consciences in their beds.   Whether any given banking system can be relied upon to produce this result is another question, the answer to which depends on the behaviour of its reserves.

If however the increase in aggregate wealth is not entirely due to the growth of population but partly to a growth in productivity per head, as it has been in America in recent years, the case is different.   In order to study this case properly, let us suppose that population has not increased at all, but that owing to better machinery or organisation or what not the power of every individual to produce goods and services has doubled.   If the supply of money is kept constant, the shopkeepers and so forth will find that in order to get rid of the increased stream of goods they have to lower their prices by one-half.   The value of the monetary unit has doubled, and so therefore has the aggregate value of the unchanged stock of chequeries in the hands of the public.   But this increase in the aggregate value of their chequeries does not represent any new act of saving on their part—it is the mere reflection or registration of the increase in their productivity. If therefore in these circumstances the bank adds to its loans in such wise as to prevent the price-level from falling, it will not be putting new spontaneous saving of the public at the disposal of industry, as it does when it expands its loans to match an increase in thrift or a growth in population.   On the contrary, if it keeps the price-level stable in these circumstances, the bank will be extracting forced savings from the public no less than if, in normal circumstances, it expands the supply of money in such a way as to drive prices upwards.[1]

[1] If, indeed, the bank can make its new loans in such a way as to do nothing but raise immediately the money incomes of all existing active workers, the enforced saving will be confined to those depositors who are

Thus in this instance, for the first time in our analysis, the action required from the bank in order to put at the disposal of trade and industry just so much new saving, and no more, as the public are disposed to make through its agency, turns out to be different from the action required from it in order to keep the general price-level stable. We need not attempt to decide at the moment which of these two courses of action is the *right* one for the bank to pursue: but once more we may well feel doubtful whether a banking system which is tied by fixed rules about its reserves will in fact be able effectively to pursue either.

§ 6. Bank Loans and the Needs of Trade.

Our doubts about the working of these reserve-rules have now become so insistent that we may well turn aside at this point to consider a proposal which is sometimes put forward by the countless orators and pamphleteers who share these doubts, and who are never tired of asserting that the first business of a banking system is to be 'responsive to the needs of industry and trade.' This proposal seems to be nothing less than this—that every person who can show reason to suppose that he is going to be able to sell £1000 worth of goods within some reasonable space of time should be entitled to borrow £1000 from the bank.

It is not difficult to put this proposal in a plausible form. Let us take a very simple instance. Suppose that two gentlemen, Mr. Eggman and Mr. Orangeman, arrive in this country by aeroplane from opposite directions, one with nothing but a couple of eggs in his pocket and the other with nothing but a couple of oranges: and that the current price of both eggs and oranges is 6d. each. Suppose that each airman, after eating half his ration, would be glad to exchange the remainder for the surplus ration of the other; but that they are too civilised and well trained in modern business methods to effect

creditors of Governments and companies, etc. (p. 10), and who, on one view, may be held not to deserve a windfall which would otherwise accrue to them. But this may be very difficult to effect: and the question of equity, which is discussed further in Ch. VII, § 1, is not clear.

a direct exchange.   Nothing can be more reasonable than that they should knock at the door of the nearest bank, and by brandishing their wares in the banker's face persuade him to create for each of them a chequery of 6d.   They then exchange cheques for 6d. in mutual payment for their wares, and each promptly repays his loan to the bank.   Everybody is satisfied. The two airmen have been saved from starving in the midst of plenty: the rest of the country carries on its business unperturbed, for the appalling slump which might otherwise have occurred in the egg and orange markets has been avoided: and the bank has performed its duty of oiling the wheels of trade— and perhaps gets the eggshell and the orange-peel as a reward. The proposal of the 'needs of trade' party seems to be justified.

Unfortunately, however, it is equally easy to put the objection to the proposal plausibly.   Suppose now that Mr. Orangeman is not an airman at all, but a local hawker, so that his orange does not, like Mr. Eggman's egg, constitute a net addition to the volume of goods in the country.   And suppose that only Mr. Eggman borrows from the bank in order to effect his purchase.   It will then be possible for Mr. Orangeman to pay Mr. Eggman's cheque into the bank, and draw *of his own right* a cheque for the same amount with which to purchase Mr. Eggman's egg.   Let us see what has happened in this case. The volume of bank-loans and the flow of exchangeable goods (reckoned at prices hitherto current) have both been increased by 6d.: but the flow of available money has been increased by 1s.—namely, by two cheques of 6d. each.   The stability of trade and prices has been upset; for whereas Mr. Orangeman's increased money demand for eggs has been offset by an increased supply of eggs, Mr. Eggman's increased money demand for oranges has not been offset by an increased supply of oranges: and the price of oranges will therefore tend to rise.

Now let us carry our illustration one stage further.   Suppose that Mr. Eggman, having raised his loan, buys Mr. Orangeman's orange as before, but puts his egg into cold storage and refuses to sell it.   Mr. Orangeman will then use his chequery to buy

(say) a packet of cigarettes from his neighbour Mr. Tobaccoman, and Mr. Tobaccoman in turn will buy a loaf from Mr.
Breadman, and so on, and so on. The chequery originated
by Mr. Eggman's loan will change its habitation not once (as
in our first case) nor twice (as in our second case), but many
times.

Now on the face of it it is the third and final version of this
story which corresponds most closely to the conditions of real
life. For the man who wants to borrow from a bank does not
as a rule resemble our original pair of airmen, who had goods
ready for sale, but were hung up by a mere mechanical difficulty.
He is a man whose products are *not* ready for immediate sale.
If he is a shopkeeper they are in his show window, if he is an
importing merchant they are on the sea, if he is a farmer they
are still in the ground, if he is an inventor they are still in his
brain: it is all a question of degree. In any case while the
goods are coming to birth, the money created on the strength
of them is going on its travels, flitting from chequery to
chequery

> Like the wandering dove which found
> No repose on earth around:

and everywhere it perches it tends to raise prices, by increasing
the willingness of somebody to buy goods. The longer the
products take in coming to birth, the more damage will the
money have time to do; thus we are led to suspect an especial
danger about loans which, as the banker puts it, 'tie up his
money' for long periods—though as we have seen it is really
the goods which are tied up and not the money, which is very
much untied and 'runs about the city.'

Clearly we are not likely to reach a precise answer along
these lines; but we have seen enough to suspect that the
validity of the claim of the 'needs of trade' party is somehow
bound up with two things—our old friend the velocity of
circulation of money, and something which we may call the
average period of production of goods. And by making one
more rather intense intellectual effort we shall find that we are

able both to express a more precise opinion on the soundness
of this particular claim, and to sum up a good deal of what we
have learnt in the earlier sections of this chapter.

§ **7. Circulating Capital.**   Let us begin, as usual, with a country
which is stationary in population and wealth.   There is in
such a country at any moment a great mass of *unready* goods,
on which labour and ingenuity of various kinds have been
spent, but which are not yet ripe for the consumer's hands or
mouth.   This mass of *circulating capital*, as it is called, includes
not only the stocks of shirts in the shop-window and the stocks
of raw cotton in the warehouses and ships, but the half-worked
fabric on its way through the spindles and the looms.   Indeed
it includes some things, such as the coal used in the factories
and the arsenic used in killing the boll-weevil, which never
reach the consumer's hands at all; and some, such as the play
which has been rehearsed but not yet performed and the lecture
which has been prepared but not yet delivered, which it takes
the eye of faith to see.

The amount of this circulating capital in existence depends
partly on the size of the annual flow of goods and services
which we call the 'real national income' (p. 29), and partly on
the speed with which, on the average, goods are made ready
for the consumer's use, or in other words on the length of
what we have just called the *average period of production of
goods*.   If for simplicity we may assume that the expenditure
of labour on the goods takes place at an even rate, we can say
that the circulating capital in existence is equal in value to
one-half the output during a period of production.   If, for
instance, we conceive of the process of production as a vast
sausage-machine which it takes ten minutes to traverse, and
which turns out one sausage per minute, one of the potential
sausages in the machine will have been there for nine minutes
and one only for one: but on the average they will have been
there for five minutes, and their average value is that which is
imparted by five minutes' laceration, i.e. the value of half a
completed sausage.   The aggregate value of the ten amorphous

objects is therefore that of five completed sausages, that is, of five minutes' output.

In connection with this figure of one-half, it will be convenient to clear out of the way a tiresome little point of arithmetic and banking technique. We supposed in § 1 that the bank gave its help to the farmer in the form of what is called a loan in the strict sense—that is to say, that it placed £1000 immediately at his disposal, so that its deposits were immediately swollen by that amount. This is the common practice in America and in London; but we might equally well have supposed that the bank proceeded by the method which is common in other parts of Great Britain, and which is known as the method of overdraft. In this case the bank would still have given the farmer the right to draw cheques up to £1000, but until the cheques were actually drawn and paid into other people's accounts, no sign of the transaction would have appeared in its balance-sheet. Assuming the farmer to make his purchases at an even rate, we see that under either system the *average* amount for which he stands *really* indebted to the bank over the period is £500 and not £1000; for under the loan system he is in effect always re-lending to the bank part of what he has borrowed from it. With the merchant it is a little different, for he must have all his £1000 at once if it is to be of any use to him: but he too, thanks to his gradual unloading of the apples, is *on the average* only really in debt to the extent of £500. We may take it then that when the 'needs of trade' party claim that a man should be entitled to borrow up to the full selling value of the goods which he intends to put on the market, what they mean is that he should be entitled to be in debt to the bank on the average for half that amount—that is for the value of the whole of his circulating capital.

§ **8. The Four Crucial Fractions.** To return to the main thread. Let us begin by supposing that this circulating capital has been built up entirely by means of bank loans, and that the saving embodied in it has been entirely provided, in the manner suggested in § 1, by the depositors of the bank, who at some time in the past have decided to refrain from exercising their full legal rights of consumption, and whose thrifty intentions have been translated into effective action by the bank. And let us further suppose that the bank has used all the resources under its control, except those provided by its own shareholders, in promoting the creation of circulating capital, having no other assets except its loans to traders and producers to set against its liabilities to its depositors. Thus the real aggregate value of the public's chequeries is exactly equal to the real aggregate value of the circulating capital. Now we know (p. 29) that the former can be expressed as a fraction of the annual national income; and we now see that the latter also can be expressed as such a fraction, that fraction being one-half the proportion which the period of production bears to a year. For instance, if the period of production is a whole year, the circulating capital is worth six months' income. Thus for equilibrium to exist, the real value of the public's chequeries must also be that of six months' income—in other words, money must circulate in final purchase of goods and services twice a year; that is, twice during a period of production. What is the bearing of this conclusion on the claims of the 'needs of trade' party? In a stationary country such as we are now considering, all new loans are 'replacement' loans of the type examined in § 2; and under the conditions set out it will therefore be quite in order for any borrower to raise the whole of the funds required to build up his circulating capital from the bank. Such a proceeding will not upset equilibrium in any way. And remembering what was said in § 5 about a country where population is growing at an even rate, we can see that in such a country too the claims of the 'needs of trade' party would still, so long as the remaining conditions which we have laid down are satisfied, be perfectly justified.

Now let us vary these conditions by assuming that only one-half of the resources controlled by the banks are embodied in circulating capital, the remainder being embodied in fixed

capital, loans to Governments, handsome neo-classical buildings, and reserves; and that only one-half of the circulating
capital has been built up by means of bank loans, the remainder
having been built up by the owners of businesses (whether they
be private individuals or the owners of joint-stock companies)
out of their own resources. Under such conditions (which
perhaps approximately represent those which prevail in
England) if any individual borrower, even in a stationary or
steadily growing community, attempts to raise the *whole* of
his circulating capital by means of bank loans, he will be
upsetting the conditions of equilibrium and leading to the
imposition of forced saving on the public.

To put the matter in a more general way. The amount of
saving which the public wish to do in monetary form and the
amount of circulating capital which industry requires are
determined by entirely separate and independent forces, the
one mainly psychological in nature and the other mainly
technical. Even in a stationary or steadily progressing community harmony is only established between them as the
result, on the one hand of a set of customs among bankers as
to the uses to which they put the resources entrusted to their
charge, on the other hand of a set of customs as to the extent
to which traders and industrialists have recourse to the banks
for their requirements of circulating capital. This delicate
equilibrium would be upset by conceding to the trader the
right to come to the bank for a loan sufficient to provide the
whole of the circulating capital which he requires. Given
the velocity of circulation of money, this upset will be greater
the longer is the period of production: and given the length
of the period of production, it will be greater the greater is
the velocity of circulation of money.

And if this is true of 'replacement' loans, or of those which
are the symptoms of a process of steady growth, it is still
more true of any loan which represents a departure from
normal conditions. If population is growing at an increasing
rate, or if an attempt is being made to speed on development
at a faster rate than the growth of population, or if an abnormal

proportion of resources is being devoted to goods whose period of production is longer than the average, a banking system which tries to respond with alacrity to 'the needs of trade' will in any case find itself in grave danger of imposing forced saving on the public; and if it attempts to supply *the whole* requirements of its clients for circulating capital, that danger will become a certainty.[1]

[1] The reader who is helped rather than frightened by the use of symbols will do well to turn to App. B: other readers are advised to read the last two sections over again.

CHAPTER VI

MONEY IN THE GREAT MUDDLE

I. MONETARY COLLAPSE

'And thick and fast they came at last,
And more, and more, and more.'
Through the Looking-glass

§ **1. The Causes of the Expansion of Money Supplies.** The reader will probably by now be disposed to concede that even in ordinary times the task of the framers of monetary policy is not a very easy one. And in the age in which we live it is rendered harder than usual by the fact that in the years following 1914 the world's monetary affairs, like the rest of its affairs, passed through a period of intense dislocation and disorder. It is beyond the scope of this book to present any detailed or connected narrative of the monetary events of those years in the several countries concerned: but there are two reasons why we cannot absolve ourselves from attempting to form some mental picture of the features of the period as a whole. In the first place, such periods of violent upheaval exhibit very clearly certain peculiar forces acting on the value of money which are at work also in periods of milder change, but which, in order to make our task manageable, we found it convenient in Chapter II to pass over in silence. Secondly, while the events about to be surveyed have now passed for the most part into the realm of history, they have, as indicated above, left behind them a legacy of heavy stones to bruise further the already battered feet of the walkers in the paths of monetary policy.

The main feature of the first half of the period was an

enormous expansion, in almost every country, of the supply of money. In the belligerent countries this expansion had its origin in the needs of the Governments concerned, which in their attempt to secure control of resources for the prosecution of the war found sooner or later that they had reached the limit of what could be done in the way of taxation or straightforward borrowing, and were obliged to have recourse to the imposition of forced saving on the public, in the manner described in Chapter V, § 3, by the issue of additional money. Nor did the needs of Governments come to an end with the restoration of what was called peace. In some countries the spirit of revolution was abroad, while in others the curious belief prevailed that the vast damage wrought by the war would somehow make it easier to maintain a far higher standard of life than had ever existed in the past: so threats had to be bought off, and illusions fostered. For a time too it almost seemed as though half mankind sat in offices, drawing salaries at the public expense for spying on the other half, who were part idling and part unemployed. Further, the French had to pay for the wanton damage done by the Germans in time of war, and the Germans a few years later had to pay for the wanton damage done by the French in time of peace. The Russians had to fight the other Russians with one hand, and to inaugurate the millennium with the other. The British had to restore order in Ireland, and the Poles to create chaos in Eastern Europe—two processes whose features were less dissimilar than might be supposed. Everybody was in debt to everybody else: and above all everybody had run up an immense account with the great Sir Galahad of the West, whose bill did not seem to be any the smaller because his heart was pure. They were great days: it is to be hoped we shall not see their like again.

But it was not only in the belligerent countries that the supply of money was expanded. For in their necessity almost all of them suspended such provisions as had been in force regarding the convertibility of their money into gold, and sent their gold in payment for what they needed to neutral countries, where it became the base for an immense pyramid of notes and bank money. Thus between 1914 and 1919 gold itself lost half its value. Further, the dire needs of the war-makers, coupled with certain powers which they possessed of making themselves unpleasant on the high seas, exercised a strong pressure on the bankers in neutral countries to expand their loans beyond all normal proportion to their reserves, in order to facilitate the supply of the goods which the war-makers needed. Thus in the end nearly all of the neutral countries also fell away from the gold standard.

§ 2. The Expansion of Bank Money in England.

The machinery of money-expansion differed in different countries. On the Continent, where common money was still of predominant importance, such money was paid out directly in exchange for the goods and services which the Government needed. Where the Government was itself an issuer of notes, this could be done without going through the form of borrowing from private persons: but where, as was more usual, the issue of notes was in the hands of one or more banks, the Government had to borrow from the banks the notes which it required. Thus between the outbreak of war and November, 1923, the note-issue of the Reichsbank increased from about two thousand million marks to about one hundred and eighty million million million marks. It will, however, be more profitable for us to examine briefly the mechanism employed during the war in England, which, while not differing in its essential nature from that employed elsewhere, was slightly more complicated and therefore slightly better calculated to throw dust into the eyes of the unsuspecting.

The mainspring of this mechanism was the Government's chequery at the Bank of England. For the Bank of England is the Government's banker, and it is quite usual for the Government to borrow moderate amounts from it in anticipation of the receipts from taxes. In ordinary times these 'Ways and Means Advances,' as they are called, are all paid back before the end of the financial year; but during the war they were allowed to grow and grow until they reached very large dimensions. The effect of this action was very important, as will be readily understood by anybody who is clear about the subject of chequeries at the Bank of England (p. 43). Suppose the Government borrows £1,000,000 from the Bank of England in order to pay a bill of £1,000,000 for ink and stationery. The Government's chequery at the Bank of England is swollen by £1,000,000 and on this chequery it draws a cheque for £1,000,000, which it pays to the stationer, who pays it into his bank, which pays it into its chequery at the Bank of England. The swelling has vanished from the Government's chequery, but has reappeared in that of the joint-stock bank. Now this bank, it will be remembered, treats its chequery as part of its reserves for purposes of the proportion of reserves to deposits which it feels bound to keep. Finding its reserves and deposits both swollen by £1,000,000, and the proportion of reserves to deposits therefore increased, it will see a chance, conformably with its own rules, of increasing its loans by an amount equal to several times the £1,000,000 originally borrowed by the Government:[1] and the upward thrust given to prices will be correspondingly magnified.

These new loans of the banks were made partly to the business world, which was busy with Government contracts, partly to the Government itself in the form of the purchase of War Loan, and partly to the public to enable them also to become purchasers of War Loan—the pieces of paper representing the Government's obligation being then lodged with the Bank as security for the bank loan. For it must be explained that the English banker when he makes a loan likes when possible to have within his clutches something of value which he can sell if the loan goes wrong. Now nothing is better 'collateral,' as it is called, than Government securities: and it is probable, though the available statistics are not sufficient to enable us to prove it, that the abundance of this good collateral induced the bankers to be somewhat more lax

[1] The reader is advised to refresh his memory of the argument on pp. 76–77.

in their views about the proper proportion of reserves to deposits than they had been before the war. And there was another cause impelling them in the same direction. A considerable part of their own loans to the Government took the form of what are called Treasury Bills, which fall due for repayment at the end of a few months; so that the banks held at any moment a mass of securities which they could force the Government to redeem with a cheque on the Bank of England if they wished to replenish their reserves.

How can we but be sorry for the English banker? Here was this Odysseus, who in his instinctive horror of the voices of the 'needs of trade' Sirens had bound himself to the mast of Proportional Reserve and sealed his ears with the wax of Good Collateral. And suddenly the mast rose from its socket and wafted him towards the dreaded voices; the wax became a perfect conductor of sound. Those things which should have been for his wealth became unto him an occasion of falling. It was his very terror of the excessive creation of money which led him to become such a willing accomplice, with the Government on the outbreak of war and with the trading community on the outbreak of peace, in a tremendous orgy of money-creation.

§ 3. The Expansion of Common Money in England. But how, it may be asked, could the banks create with safety these additional supplies of bank money? For it will be remembered that though the particular rules adopted by bankers about their reserves may be arbitrary, they have their roots in the very solid fact that bank money is convertible, and that since the people of this country prefer to make a considerable part of their payments in common money, a good deal of bank money is actually presented for conversion. Either the actual borrowers of additional bank loans, or those to whom they make payments, generally require to use part of their increased purchasing power for the hire of additional labour, or the making of overtime payments to their existing staffs. For this purpose they must obtain additional common money from the bank: and the bank knows that such a request for additional common money is bound to result sooner or later from the making of additional loans.

Further, while the influence of additional loans manifests itself first on the wholesale prices of staple goods, by increasing the ability of the business classes to buy, it does not stop there. With greater or less speed it communicates itself to the retail prices of common things, not so much, in the first instance, by increasing the ability of buyers to buy, as by increasing the reluctance of sellers to sell.   A manufacturer who has bought yarn dear will not, if he can help it, sell cloth to tailors cheap. A wholesale merchant who has bought cheese at 1s. 6d. a lb. will not, if he can help it, let the village grocer have it for 1s. 3d.

And from this process of the rise of retail prices two consequences follow.   First, those who have cheque-books find that they require to keep on their persons a larger amount of common money—perhaps even to keep a larger proportion of their resources in the form of common money; for they must economise, if at all, in the things which are usually paid for by cheque, such as motor-cars.   Secondly, and more important, the wage-earners make efforts to get their money wages raised to cope with the increased cost of living.   During the years 1917–20, these efforts were singularly insistent and successful, with the result of a great increase in the quantity of common money required each week from the banks for the payment of wages.

It follows that with the best will in the world to support either British arms or British trade, the banks could not afford to forget the effect which additional loans would have in the near future on the requisitions of the business community for common money: or if they did permit themselves to forget it, the course of events soon jogged their memory.   How then was the common money to be supplied?   To the extent that the banks were holders of Treasury Bills, they were enabled in effect to shunt off the responsibility for finding the necessary supplies of common money on to the Government.   And to the extent that they found their chequeries at the Bank of

8

England swollen as a consequence of the making of Ways and Means Advances, they were enabled to shunt off the responsibility on to the Bank of England. Now the Bank of England showed itself very accommodating in these years about the proportion which it kept between its reserves (which were all old-fashioned legal tender) and its deposits: but all the same, it could not run the risk of being unable to fulfil its obligation of providing the banks with common money as and when they required it. So by one route or another the responsibility for finding the necessary supplies of common money came in the last resort upon the only body which *can* create common money at will—the Government. The situation then was this —that unless the Government was prepared to let the whole banking system go smash—indeed, unless it was prepared to default on its own Treasury Bills—it had to be ready to create so much common money as might be called for by any loan policy which it permitted the banking system to pursue.

We see therefore yet a third way in which the very conservatism of the English banking system enabled it, in changed conditions, to run riot in the manufacture of money. For any arrangement which would keep them well supplied with common money was good enough for the joint-stock banks, and any arrangement which would enable it to meet its obligations, while keeping a reserve of decent size and old-fashioned composition, was good enough for the Bank of England.

The actual arrangement by which these happy results were achieved—by which Treasury Notes made their début into the world—is interesting as furnishing one more example of the adaptability of the device of chequery keeping at the Bank of England. The Treasury Note Department, like so many other people, indulged in this convenient habit; and when a bank wanted additional Treasury Notes, it bought them by drawing a cheque on the Bank of England which reduced its own chequery there, and swelled that of the Treasury Note Department by an equal amount. This swelling was thereupon transferred to the Government's ordinary chequery—the Right Hand of the Government, so to speak, borrowed from its Left, using the resulting increase in its chequery to make its own purchases, and leaving the Left Hand with a bundle of promises to pay instead of a nice fat chequery of its own.

There has been some controversy about the exact part played by the Treasury Notes in connection with the great war-rise of prices in England. It will be seen from the account given above that that part can best be described by saying that the knowledge, on the part of somebody, that they *could be created if necessary*, was an essential condition of the expansion of bank loans which gave the initial thrust to prices; while their actual entry into the world served to maintain a rise already achieved, by maintaining the ability of the population, and especially of the working-classes, to buy goods. And this conclusion is not of historical interest only: for the events of the war only illustrated on an abnormal scale the parts normally played by bank money and common money respectively in bringing about changes in the price-level in an Anglo-Saxon country.

§ 4. The Inter-reactions of the Conditions of Demand for and Supply of Money.

When the supply of money is expanding rapidly in this way, and prices are consequently rising and expected to continue to rise, certain curious things happen which demand our attention.

In the first place such a state of affairs is, as we have seen (p. 10), favourable to those in control of business policy, so that the output of goods is stimulated and the rise in prices tends to be held in check. In the war, however, this tendency was entirely overborne by the numerous and obvious forces operating to restrict the output of goods; so that for this reason alone the rise in prices would have tended to outstrip the expansion in the supply of money.

There is, however, a more important way in which a continuing increase in the supply of money affects the conditions of demand for it (p. 32). As the new money gets into circulation, the members of the public find their holdings of money increasing: and being accustomed to think in terms of money and not of real things, they try to reduce their holdings of money to the normal level by spending them faster. Thus the velocity of circulation of money increases. Later, when they come to give the matter conscious thought, many members of the public, especially those whose incomes are fixed in money and who are therefore suffering particularly from the rise in prices, come to ask themselves whether they were not keeping command over an unnecessarily large proportion of their real income in the form of money, and whether they cannot to some extent mitigate their privations by being less cautious in this respect. Thus the increase in the velocity of circulation of money, at first the result of lack of thought, becomes deliberate. Finally, if the expansion of the supply of money proceeds to extravagant lengths, the public lose confidence in the money altogether. Use it they must, if there is no other: but every individual passes it on as quickly as he is able, knowing that if he keeps it it will lose value still further on his hands, and seeks with ingenuity and persistence to embody his resources rather in any other form. If he is an industrialist, he will know how to turn them into bricks and mortar and machines; whence the paradox that in 1922-3, when masses of the population of Germany were being driven towards starvation and despair by the cataclysmic fall in the value of money, her captains of industry entered into possession of a large and magnificent new treasure of industrial equipment. The private individual must be content with pictures, jewels, clothes, kitchen utensils; but something that will last a little, and that is not money, he will do his level best to find.

Thus the velocity of circulation becomes hectic, and prices rise out of all proportion to the increase in the stock of money. And the faster they rise, the more money the Government needs, and the less distance do taxes, fixed on the basis of what money was worth only a few weeks previously, go towards meeting its needs. So the creation of money receives a new impetus: the very fact that the demand for it has *diminished*, by a bewildering but perfectly natural paradox, stimulates the expansion of the supply. The thunder and lightning—the price-level and the money-supply—go chasing each other about the room, knocking over the tables and things as in the White Queen's story: and no one knows how it will all end.

And this same fact—that expectation is always outrunning actuality—produces another complication. While the income-value of money falls quite fast enough, its transaction-value falls still faster: for capital equipment and raw materials and finished goods at wholesale change hands at prices determined by what people think that goods at retail will be worth a few weeks hence. Thus every business man who forms a link in the chain of production and sale has an interest in bringing pressure to bear that the expected rise in retail prices may materialise, and that the engine of money creation may not be reversed.[1]

§ 5. The Misbehaviour of the Foreign Exchanges. There is also in many cases a further reason why the prices of materials rise out of proportion to the rise in the prices of ready goods and services—a reason connected with the foreign exchanges. In Chapter IV, § 3, we examined the underlying forces which, under relatively stable conditions, determine the price of foreign money: but we must never forget that in the case of foreign money, as of other things (p. 32), the only *proximate* forces determining its price at any moment are the willingness of buyers to buy and the willingness of sellers to sell. Now if a country is rapidly increasing its supply of money, the same lack of confidence in the future of the money which ultimately worms its way into the skull of the thickest-headed citizen, strikes like a flash upon the consciousness of the well-informed and impressionable gentlemen whose business it is to carry on dealings in foreign money. They become highly willing to buy foreign money and to sell the money of their own country. Further, as ordinary citizens of substance become aware of what is happening to their own money, they do their best to transfer their savings to other countries; and this involves their coming on to the exchange market as purchasers of foreign money. And if the Government has big payments to make abroad in return for imports needed to keep its people from

[1] Those with strong digestions may like to turn to App. A, II.

starvation or revolution, or in satisfaction of the claims of foreign Governments (and of the German Government *par excellence* both these things were true in the post-war years), it, too, adds a heavy weight to the same side of the scales. Thus the price of foreign money soars upward out of proportion to the price of goods and services produced at home. Indeed, there is theoretically no limit to what at any moment it may attain.[1]   For suppose, to use our old puppets, people in Utopia simply must acquire claims to £1 million in England in a particular week in order to meet their debts: and suppose that the claims to pounds arising out of the sale of Utopian goods, etc., in England and available for purchase in Utopia amount only to £$\frac{3}{4}$ million.   Competition to obtain this £$\frac{3}{4}$ million will drive up the price of the pound: but however many utopes the Utopians offer for the £$\frac{3}{4}$ million available, they will still be short by £$\frac{1}{4}$ million of the sum needed to meet their obligations.

One temporary expedient may indeed be open to them—to find Englishmen who are foolish enough actually to buy and import Utopian common money in the belief that it must some day rise again in value.   In the early days of monetary decay this may not be difficult, as the Germans found in 1919–20; but after a time the speculators lose heart, and the tide sets heavily the other way.   And even while this expedient remains open, equilibrium of any kind is only reached provided there is *some* price at which the owners of pounds are ultimately willing to part with them for utopes.   Otherwise the Utopians must either borrow the pounds, if they can find anyone to lend to them, or declare themselves in default.   Thus a falling exchange is not, as it seemed sometimes to be thought to be in the countries concerned, a device by which those countries could, as it were, make terms with fate and earn the right to be extravagant—a kind of magical composition-fee for enabling a nation to spend too much without getting into debt.

§ 6. The Divergence between Internal and External Price-levels.

And now how do these antics of the exchanges affect the price

[1] Bickerdike, *Economic Journal*, March 1920.

of goods? The price of imported goods will tend to move directly and exactly with the price of foreign money—to reflect the degree of confidence felt in the future of the country's money by the nimble-witted dealers in exchange rather than that felt by the average stolid member of the home population. True, especially if the imports consist largely of food and raw materials, the price of home-produced goods and services will come lumbering after: for the money costs of production and of living will be raised, and those who suffer from this rise will exert a strong pressure on the Government and the banks to speed on with the expansion of the money supply. But the gap between the *external* and the *internal value* of money, as the technical phrase goes, is likely to remain unclosed unless and until the final stage is reached in which (as happened in Austria and Germany) the inhabitants of the country, at last utterly disillusioned about their own money, conduct even their everyday retail dealings in terms of some relatively stable foreign money.

But how, the reader will ask, can these things be? Have we not learnt in Chapter IV, § 3, that if the prices of foreign money and of imports misbehave in this way, the flow of imports will be checked and the flow of exports stimulated until those prices of foreign money and of imports are again established which the existing money supply of the country, as compared with that of other countries, renders permanently maintainable (p. 60)? And the answer is Yes, under normal conditions that is true: but the conditions we are now examining are abnormal in two ways. In the first place, it may be highly inconvenient to let the stimulus to the flow of exports work out its full effect: for to do so might be to allow the country to be denuded, under the spur of private gain, of foodstuffs and materials and items of industrial equipment which are judged essential to the maintenance of the national life. Thus the German Government, for instance, was led to intervene, by the rigid control of certain classes of exports, to prevent what was called the 'auction-sale' of Germany, and so, for what seemed to it good and sufficient reasons, to thwart the most powerful force which was operating to stem the fall in the external value of the mark.

Secondly, in Chapter IV, § 3, we were discussing conditions in which the suppliers of money, while not tied to a gold standard, are assumed capable of *independent* action; whereas under the conditions now being considered, the country's money-glands are in so highly pathological a state that, as we have seen, they are likely to be stimulated to further activity by the very movement of the prices of foreign money and of imports which it is their normal function to inhibit. Thus the country's power of purchase both over imports and over its own products will be bolstered up, and the corrective alteration in the flow of imports and exports prevented from taking place. Under such conditions, to call the rate of exchange which reflects the relative prices of traded goods the *normal* rate (p. 58) is in truth misleading: for it is *not* the rate which reflects the *existing* condition of the country's money-supply as compared with that of other countries (p. 60). Even, however, under such conditions, the actual rate of exchange is largely governed by the *expected* behaviour of the country's monetary authority; and if that authority behaves in a way which is not expected, the rate will ultimately alter. But in the meantime, besides the lightning and the thunder—the supply of money and the internal price-level—we have a third thing, the thunderbolt of the exchanges and the external price-level, tumbling about the room and puzzling us as to where exactly it fits into the sequence of cause and effect.

II. MONETARY RESTORATION

'Well, I'll eat it,' said Alice; 'and if it makes me larger I can reach the key; and if it makes me smaller, I can creep under the door; so either way I'll get into the garden, and I don't care which happens!'

Alice's Adventures in Wonderland

§ 7. The Pinning of the Exchanges. Such things as these happened in most countries, in greater or less degree, during

the years of the Great Muddle.   At last, though as it turned
out long before the climax was reached, a number of wise and
well-disposed men met in Brussels (1920) to give advice about
what should be done.   Several of these men had been well
trained in economic theory, and knew therefore that, whatever
the temporal sequence of events might be, the existence of a
certain state of a country's money-glands was the *essential
condition* for the continuance of a certain state of its price-
level and exchanges.   They knew too that the bad state of the
world's money-glands was due to the inordinate demands made
by Governments upon their peoples and upon each other.
The latter part of this second truth they were not allowed to
disclose; about the former part they spoke very severely,
recommending that Governments should forthwith reduce
their expenditure and balance their budgets.   Which was very
good advice, and about as much use as recommending a
drowning man to keep dry.

So the muddle went on, until the idea began to occur to
some people that if they could not kill the snake by knocking
it on the head, there might be something to be said for grasping
it firmly by the tail.   If by hook or by crook the external value
of the money could be prevented from plunging any *further*
downwards, a breathing space could be secured.   This
breathing space could be utilised in two alternative ways.
Either the internal price-level could be allowed to rise to an
equality with the external, thus allowing the Government to
sin a little more in the interval: or an attempt could be made to
pin the internal price-level at the level which it had reached,
in the hope that the exchange market, growing confident that
something was really being done at last, would revise the
valuation which it put upon the country's money, thus enabling
the price of foreign money to be ultimately fixed at a somewhat
lower level than that at which it had originally been held.   The
consequences of these two alternative lines of action will be
examined later: but whichever of them, or whatever compromise between the two, was adopted, there remained another
circumstance making the path of virtue, once it had been

firmly entered by the wrong end, somewhat easier to follow than might have been feared. Once confidence could be restored by determined action of any kind the forces increasing the velocity of circulation of money (p. 98) were violently reversed—the desire of the population to hold command over resources in the convenient form of money was easily fanned once more into flame. Thus the Government could repeat St. Augustine's prayer, 'Make me pure, but not yet,' with every chance of being heard: it could go on for a while expanding the money supply to discharge its urgent obligations without driving up in proportion the level of internal prices.

§ 8. The Machinery of Stabilisation.

The pre-requisite for putting this short-circuiting method into operation was a stock of foreign money, by selling which to all comers at the chosen rate the Government could brazen it out that all would yet be well. In the case of Austria, the earliest country to adopt the method (1922), the foreign money was provided out of loans guaranteed by foreign Governments and arranged by the League of Nations, which for this piece of pioneer work alone would deserve the gratitude of mankind. Some other countries (such as Hungary) had recourse later to the aid of the same good fairy; but others (such as Belgium) were able to raise public foreign loans unaided, while others again (such as France) found it sufficient to make private arrangements with powerful foreign financial groups. Here again, notably in France, the path of virtue proved easier than might have been feared: for, so soon as some measure of confidence was restored, those persons who had succeeded in transferring their savings to foreign lands (p. 99) proved reasonably willing to sell their foreign possessions to their own Government in return for its money, thus assisting it to build up a store of money abroad. In Germany, supplies of foreign money were ultimately obtained by loan under the provisions of the Dawes Plan (1924), which also performed the indispensable task of limiting the pressure on the exchange market caused by the Government's liability to make payments for reparation of war damage (p. 100). But nine months before this date, Germany had already knocked the snake somewhere about the middle of the body by applying with triumphant success a plan which flew in the face of all the teachings of history and of theory. She introduced a brand new money, 'based' (a word of blessed vagueness) on the aggregate land and other property of Germany, and redeemable into paper claims to a share in the income of that property. This device, on the face of it idiotic, made a successful psychological appeal, especially to the dominant agricultural party: but even so it was, of course, only made to work by the fact that the supply of the 'renten-marks' was resolutely restricted by the authorities in charge.

Russia alone received to the last no foreign aid. Her Government was obliged to build up its stores of foreign money by careful management of its monopoly of foreign trade, and eased its own path to the heights of virtue by conducting for a year the unique experiment of a true double standard. A new money, the chervonetz, whose external value was kept stable, was issued by the State Bank, while the Treasury itself continued to satisfy its own needs by pouring out the old roubles on to the market; and for a year (1923) the two moneys circulated side by side, with a continually varying rate of exchange between them.

The foreign money which was elected to be thus stabilised in price was as a rule the dollar; and as the dollar had retained throughout its original value in terms of gold, this involved the restoration of a gold standard. When therefore the price at which the dollar was to be held had been finally determined, there remained the formal step of re-defining the weight of gold to the value of which the value of the money was to be kept equal. In most cases this step followed quickly, though in the case of France it was long delayed owing to the necessity to France (or more strictly to M. Poincaré) that M. Poincaré should first be given another three years' lease of office (1928). The method of re-definition differed in different countries. Sometimes a wholly new monetary unit was invented: thus the European Zoo is now enriched by a number of species—

the lit and the lat, the Polish zloty and the Hungarian pengo
—which were unknown to our ancestors.　In other cases, such
as France and Italy, the old unit was retained, but the weight
of gold to whose value its value was to be kept equal was fixed
afresh, in the former instance at about a fifth, in the latter at
rather more than a quarter of the pre-war weight.　But the
rouble and the mark were declared to be worth as much gold
as ever they were in their palmiest days: and there is nothing
in the exchange quotations to remind us of the dreadful truth
that on one fine day in February, 1924, a new rouble was
declared to be fair exchange for fifty thousand million pre-war
roubles, and on one fine day in August of the same year a new
Reichsmark was declared to be fair exchange for no less than
a million million pre-war marks.

The method of short-circuit, while it rendered the task of
Governments in balancing their budgets no longer hopeless,
did not, of course, get rid of the need for that task ultimately
to be performed.　Where the Good Fairy of Geneva had
intervened with handfuls of foreign money, she also, taking
on (as fairies will, for our good) the disguise of a disagreeable
old woman, intervened to see that economy was practised and
financial equilibrium restored.　Other Governments applied
the penitential lash to their own backs: and in either case the
process was charged with much unmerited suffering for many
worthy officials, who were roughly torn from office stools of
which they seemed to have grown almost a part.　And there
was another indispensable task to be performed.　An appreciable proportion of the debt of most Governments was
in the form of short-term obligations which, like the English
Treasury Bills, were constantly knocking at the door for
repayment: and so long as this situation persisted, it might at
any time be necessary to set the money-glands to work again
in order to repay them.　It was necessary therefore either to
pay them off for good and all, or to persuade the holders to
exchange them for promises to pay at some more remote date.
In Italy, persuasion took the simple form of an announcement that the desired exchange had taken place.　Belgium,

out-Mussolini-ing Mussolini, gave the holders the option of being repaid in the Government's own good time or of accepting preference shares in the newly formed State railway company. France adopted the more humdrum methods of voluntary conversion and of repayment out of the proceeds of taxation and reparation receipts.

§ **9. The Effects of Stabilisation on Industry.**   More important than these differences in procedure were the differences in the answer given to the fundamental question—whether to stabilise finally at the rate of exchange already reached, or to aim ultimately at a rate reflecting more faithfully the less demoralised *internal* value of the money concerned.   For the nature of this answer had important effects on general business conditions both in the country concerned and in other countries as well.   So long as in any country the price of foreign money is rising faster than the price of goods and services produced at home, those in control of its exporting industries are in receipt of an artificial stimulus: for their costs of production are not rising so fast as the proceeds of the sale of the foreign money which they are receiving abroad in payment for their goods.   They can thus afford to raise the prices of their goods, reckoned in home money, and yet to sell at lower prices, reckoned in foreign money, than their rivals in other countries. If it is now decided to stabilise the money at its lower (external) value, this artificial advantage is gradually, but only gradually, obliterated: while the industries making for home consumption are stimulated by the rise in internal prices which this decision entails.   If on the other hand it is decided to stabilise the money at its higher (internal) value, the artificial advantage of the export trades is cut off as with a knife, to the great delight of their rivals in other countries: while those in control of home industries are, except so far as they had counted on a still *further* rise of internal prices, left comparatively unaffected. The former and less drastic policy was adopted (1926) in Belgium, the latter in France, where public opinion rightly refused to accept the panic depths reached by the franc on the exchange market in the summer of 1926 as representing its 'true' value. Where the latter policy was chosen, it was dictated largely by the need to have regard to the interests of the holders of Government debt—in France a particularly numerous and important class; for such persons, as we have seen (p. 10), are damaged by a rise in the internal price-level. In every country a compromise had to be arrived at between doing their claim full justice and striking off the shackles which it imposed on the limbs of monetary reform and industrial recovery. In Germany the Government's creditors were totally disregarded and ruined, though an attempt was made later to dole out to them a consolatory pittance. In Italy they fared better than at one time seemed at all likely: for Mussolini, not content to stabilise the lira at its higher (internal) value, dragged that value upward by a drastic and painful contraction of the money supply before finally (1927) pinning it to gold.

It was not to every country that the problem of choice between a higher and a lower value for its money presented itself in the form described above. For while as a rule, for the reasons given in § 5, the external value of a country's money falls faster than the internal, this rule admits of exceptions. If in any country monetary decay has not proceeded very far, and if there is a confident belief in the minds of the dealers in exchange that it intends and will be able, by resolutely contracting its money supply, to restore the old value of its money in terms of gold, that very expectation will prevent the external value of the money from falling so fast as the internal value. This state of affairs involves an artificial handicap on those in control of the export trades, who find their receipts from the sale of foreign money rising more slowly than their costs of production. And when the country begins to turn the corner, the same relative state of affairs prevails—the external value of the money rises faster than the internal, and exporters find their receipts falling faster than their costs. If now the value of the money were to be stabilised at its lower (internal) level, the exporters would find this depressing weight

immediately removed, and the home trades would be unaffected:
while if the intention of stabilising at the higher (external)
level is piously fulfilled, the home trades have to join the export
trades in the mill of falling prices and discouragement.

There is little doubt that a situation of this kind existed in
Denmark and Norway in 1926-7, and that those countries put
their industries through a grinding mill of disenheartenment and
unemployment in order to restore the old value, in terms of
gold, of their monetary units.   As to whether such a situation
prevailed in Great Britain there has been hot dispute, turning
on the interpretation of index-numbers.   There is no question
that in the nine months preceding the restoration of the gold
standard in May, 1925, the external value of the pound, as
derived from the price of dollars, climbed far more rapidly
than the internal, under the stimulus of the belief that restoration of the gold standard at the old rate was imminent.   But
did this climb really represent a departure from equilibrium?
or did it rather represent the restoration of an equilibrium
which had prevailed till early in 1923, and had thereafter been
upset by an abnormal fall in the value of the pound in terms
of dollars, due to the general troubles of Europe in that year
and particularly to the reduced willingness of Americans to
entrust their savings to that seething cauldron?   Different
authorities have given different answers.   But it is clear that
between October, 1924, and May, 1925, the British export
trades found an increasing weight upon their shoulders *as
compared with the previous eighteen months*, and that by the
decisive act of May that weight was riveted round their necks.

§ **10. The Aftermath of Stabilisation.**   But all these things, it
will be said, have passed into history.   Whether readjustment
was brought about by patting A on the back or by hitting B in
the face can make no difference to us now.   With practically
the whole world back on a gold standard, world trade cannot
now be taking any other course than that which the true
relative needs and efficiencies of the several nations impose
upon it.   To argue thus is to underestimate the element of

play which, as has been explained (p. 66), always exists in a monetary mechanism designed to maintain a gold standard, and to underrate the forces which, after a period of violent upheaval, are at work to induce monetary authorities to use that element of play to an exceptional extent. In some countries, such as France, an exaggerated sense of the difficulty of maintaining the external value of the money may continue to check the money supply unnecessarily, and to hamper the rise of the internal price-level to its natural level. In others, such as Japan, the machinery for enforcing a contraction of the money supply upon the banks may prove inadequate. In others again, such as Great Britain and Russia, while that machinery is of exceptional power, the political and psychological obstacles to putting it into operation may prove far more serious than was anticipated. The time may come when all these complications have completely passed away: but the first readers of this book at all events can take it that the aftermath of the Great Muddle is not yet wholly reaped, and that this matter of the divergence between external and internal price-levels, and the consequent warping of the course of trade, is still among the things of which some account must be taken by the framers of monetary policy.

CHAPTER VII

THE QUESTION OF THE STANDARD

The Caterpillar was the first to speak.

'What size do you want to be?' it asked.

'Oh, I'm not particular to size,' Alice hastily replied; 'only one doesn't like changing so often, you know.'

'I *don't* know,' said the Caterpillar.

Alice's Adventures in Wonderland

§ **1. The Case for a Price-level Varying Inversely with Productive Power.** In approaching at last the theme of monetary policy, it is impossible to evade a question which many people would prefer to treat as closed. Has the world done wisely to tie itself up again in the bonds of a gold standard, or ought we to look forward to a time when that decision will be reversed? And to form an opinion on this question, we must turn our thoughts for a little to one more fundamental yet. How, if we were perfectly free to choose, should we like the value of money to behave? The natural view would seem to be that we should like its value to remain stable—that, at all events, is the natural inference from the great disturbances to contract and expectation, and so to the distribution and creation of real wealth, which follow from any violent exhibition of instability in the value of money, and which have been sufficiently emphasised in the first chapter of this book. But it is not a self-evident view: there are at least two other plausible theories of the manner in which, if we had a free hand in the matter, we ought to require the value of money to behave.

The first of these points out that the real cost, in human

9

effort and inconvenience, of producing marketable goods does not remain constant from generation to generation, or even from year to year. There are three deep-seated tendencies in human affairs which operate in modifying these real costs, the first in one direction, the other two in the other. First, the progress of invention and scientific research, of commercial and industrial organisation, of the systematic exploitation of new sources of supply, is continually operating to increase the command of man over nature, and to reduce the real cost at which goods are supplied. During the last half, and especially the last quarter, of the nineteenth century, this tendency was working almost unchecked. But, secondly, the growth of population, the limits which are set to the cultivable area of the earth and to the alacrity with which nature responds to the attentions of man, the degree to which the world is still condemned to live on its capital stores of energy (in the form of coal and oil) as contrasted with its current income—all these exert an intermittent but perhaps in the long run a gradually increasing pressure in the opposite direction. Thirdly, we cannot ignore the tendency of the nations of men to demolish, from time to time, their capital accumulations and their achievements of organisation by the waging of Wars and the elaboration of Peaces, and so to raise the real cost at which goods are forthcoming.

Now to some extent, it is argued, the operation of these tendencies is foreseen and allowed for in the making of money contracts. A man who consents to receive £100 next year, or £5 a year for ever, or whatever it may be, has made his own estimate of what changes in the productivity of human effort, and consequently in the value of money, the future will bring forth. And further, in so far as he has not done so, or in so far as his estimates are falsified by events, it is desirable that his expectations should *not* be exactly fulfilled, but that he should receive either more or less real stuff than he expected, in accordance with any unforeseen expansion or shrinkage that may take place in the productivity of human effort.

There is clearly a great deal to be said for this view.   Supposing for instance

> The world's great age begins anew
> The golden years return,
> The earth doth like a snake renew
> Her winter weeds outworn:

supposing that man continues to advance from triumph to triumph in his struggle with nature: would it not be desirable that those whose money incomes are relatively fixed by law or custom, and who are not as a rule the most self-assertive members of the community, should receive automatically a share in the fruits of progress in the form of falling prices, even though they had no definite expectation of doing so?[1]   Again, would it not be desirable that the wage-earners, though they may have proved their capacity for securing by some means or other a share of any booty that is going, should be enabled to do so without having recourse to perpetual demands for a rise in money wages—demands which, whether or not they involve actual stoppages of work, certainly tend to embitter human relations and to devour the energies of constructive leadership?

Supposing, on the other hand, that the world should fail to solve the problem of mechanical power, or that the Great War should prove to have been but the first of a series of disastrous explosions, can it be maintained that those with fixed incomes should be allowed, as would happen if prices were kept stable, to absorb always the same absolute amount, and consequently a greater proportionate amount, of society's real income of goods and services?   'I'll have my bond, speak not against my bond'—is that a plea which should be listened to from debenture-holder or trade unionist in a country shivering for lack of fuel or impoverished by chronic warfare?

It is on such grounds that a case can be made out for a standard of value which should remain stable not in terms of goods in general, but in terms of labour or productive power.

[1] Cf. Marshall, Evidence before Gold and Silver Commission, C. 5512–2, Qq 9816 ff.

And the case is very much strengthened by the conclusion at which we arrived in Chapter V, § 5, that it is by maintaining such a standard that a banking system can most easily put at the disposal of trade and industry so much, and only so much, real saving as the public are willing to do in monetary form. Even therefore if we decide on other grounds that the value of money should normally be kept stable, we should probably admit than an exception ought to be made in the event of any abnormal alteration in human productivity such as might be occasioned by the harnessing of radio-activity or a hundred years' war. And even in more ordinary conditions, in deciding *what* value of money to stabilise, we should perhaps be led to give some weight to the considerations set forth above by choosing either an index-number of the *transaction* value of money in which considerable weight is attached to wage-payments, or an index of retail prices—for goods at retail embody much labour of various kinds. We should, at all events, be sceptical of the suitability for our purpose of these index-numbers of *wholesale* prices which are still too commonly regarded as satisfactorily expressing the value of money: and we shall be interested to discover that that important and influential institution, the Federal Reserve Bank of New York, has for some years taken this view, and been working on a transaction-value index of its own.[1]

§ 2. The Case for a Gently Rising Price-level. But before committing ourselves more deeply than that, we had better consider a very different view of the way in which the value of money should behave. We have seen (p. 10) that a fall in this value, by altering the terms of old contracts in their favour, works to the advantage of those who plan and control the operation of our industrial system. And we have seen (p. 97) that a *continuing* fall in this value, by encouraging their expectations of further gains of this kind, stimulates them to an increased production of goods. There is no reason to doubt that this is true. For anyone who prides himself on being a

[1] Carl Snyder, *Harvard Review of Economic Statistics*, Feb. 1928.

'sound money' man, or is in receipt of a fixed money income, or is interested in schemes for the ideal apportionment of the fruits of industrial progress, it is convenient to forget it: but it is true all the same. A gently rising price-level pleases the business men; and the business men are in the saddle, and hold the reins of industry. The 'needs of trade' enthusiasts of the business world know, within limits, what they are about. The battle in which we defeated them in Chapter V was fought on ground of our own choosing—the ground that they must not extract forced savings from the public. But what if they say that they do not see the objection, and that they would prefer that prices should rise? We are in their hands: they are in charge of production. Nor, they may fairly urge, is this a purely selfish preference on their part, designed in the exclusive interests of 'profiteers.' Would the railways or the electrical plant of the world ever have been built if we had been afraid of a little forced saving? Is it not rising prices that empty the workhouses and the employment exchange registers, and fill the factories and the shipyards? And is it not better that all should be busy, even though grumbling at the cost of living, than that some should be living cheaply and others left on the streets?

Of course the stimulus of rising prices is partly founded in illusion. The salaried official and the trade unionist have been beguiled into accepting employment for a lower real reward than they intended. Even the business leader is the victim of illusion: for he is spurred on not only by real gains at the expense of his debenture-holders and his doctor and even (with a little luck) of his workpeople, but also by imaginary gains at the expense of his fellow business men. It is so hard at first to believe that other people will really have the effrontery or the good fortune to raise their charges as much as he has raised his own. But whether real or illusory, the spur is effective; for in economic as in other matters human endeavour feeds partly on illusion, and only partly on truth. That is why so much of the criticism levelled at the war finance of Governments falls wide of the mark. War-lords know more about morale than 'sound money' men do: it is their business.

And if conjuring tricks are indispensable in war, are we so sure than we can do without them in peace? Has any class in recent years shown itself so responsive to the stimulus of naked truth? So long as the control of production is in the hands of a minority, rewarded by means of a fluctuating profit, it is not impossible that a gently rising price-level will in fact produce the best attainable results, not only for them but for the community as a whole. And it is possible that a price-level continually falling, even for the best of reasons, would prove deficient in those stimuli upon which modern society, whether wisely or not, has hitherto chiefly relied for keeping its members in full employment and getting its work done.

On the whole, then, if we were perfectly free to choose, we should perhaps stick fairly closely to the obvious decision to keep the price-level stable. But we should force ourselves to interpret that decision with care: we should be prepared either to suspend it, or to compel the overhauling of money contracts, in exceptional circumstances: and so long at any rate as we preserve the system variously known as Private Enterprise and as Wage Slavery, we should not refuse to wink at a little judicious use of the money-pump, if the tyres of industry seemed to be sagging unduly.

§ 3. The Case against the Gold Standard.

Now let us return to the gold standard, and see whether it offers any certain prospect of guiding our course, either in our chosen *via media*, or in any of the other paths proposed. The answer must surely be that it does not. To a country with a gold standard it may happen, and it has happened, that owing to a heavy production and import of gold, the supplies of money are increased, regardless of the power of industry to make fruitful use at the moment of the resources thrust into its hands, and regardless of the burden imposed by rising prices upon ordinary folk. Or again it may happen, and it has happened, that owing to a shortage of gold reserves, the rate of increase of industrial output is retarded, though everything may be ripe for an industrial expansion, and though the public may be bubbling over with the desire and intention to save and to put its savings, if only it knew how, at the disposal of industry through the medium of the banking system.   That is the essence of the case, now hardly disputed, against the uncontrolled gold standard.

The conduct of that standard in the century before the war was indeed far from exemplary.   The behaviour of wholesale prices is, as we have seen, not a completely satisfactory test: but taking it for the moment for want of a better, we find that in England between 1821–5 and 1846–50 wholesale prices fell by 25 per cent: between 1846–50 and 1871–5 they rose by 20 per cent: between 1871–5 and 1894–8 they fell by 40 per cent: between 1894–8 and 1909–13 they rose by 30 per cent.[1]   That the gold standard provided on the whole a healthy stimulus to industry in the second of these periods is possibly true, but largely fortuitous and due to unforeseen happenings both in the diggings of California and Australia and in the banking world of London.   That by permitting a great fall in prices it reflected the great increase in the world's productivity during the third period is also true, but again partly fortuitous: and let us not forget the great agricultural decline, and the unemployment and labour ferment of the 'eighties.   For the conduct of gold in the fourth period there is very little to be said.

On the misbehaviour of gold in the years following 1914 it would not be fair to lay too much stress, any more than on any of the other economic phenomena of the Great Muddle. But it is important to get some impression of how we stand at the present time.   Roughly speaking, the world is now supporting a price-level 50 per cent higher than in 1914 with a stock of gold increased by only 40 per cent, and that in spite of the increase in population, and consequently in the demand for money, in the intervening years.   The way this has been done is of course by economising in the use of gold, and especially by the substitution of gold bullion and gold exchange for gold circulation systems.   Thus something like nine-tenths of the world's monetary stocks of gold are now concentrated

[1] Layton, *Introduction to the Study of Prices*, p. 23 (carried to 1909–13).

in Central Banks and State Treasuries, as compared with about three-fifths in 1913—the remainder being in the hands of the ordinary banks and of the people.   There are, however, ominous signs that this tendency towards gold-economy is undergoing a reversal.   In many of the Continental countries which have re-established a gold standard, not only are the laws regulating the proportion of reserves to notes very strict, but the option to hold part of the reserves in the form of foreign chequeries and securities is being decreasingly utilised. There is a disposition about to regard the gold exchange system as a mere half-way house on the road to a gold bullion or even a gold circulation system.   Indian political opinion is also clamouring for such a change: and it is probable that when China settles down, she will bring herself into line with the rest of the world by substituting some form of gold standard for her present complicated network of silver and arbitrary standards.   If these tendencies continue unchecked, a strong force may be set to work dragging down world-prices towards their pre-war level.

Against this must be set the fact that on the face of it, without altering or infringing her laws about the proportion of gold to be held against Federal Reserve notes and deposits, America could still drain off several hundreds of millions of dollars' worth of gold into the rest of the world.   But as we shall see later, it is not so easy as might appear at first sight for the American banking system to create the conditions which promote such an outflow of gold.   Supposing, however, for the moment that the redistribution of the surplus American stocks just about balances in its effects the increased tendency towards gold-hogging in the rest of the world, what of the future ?   The stock of monetary gold is at present increasing by about 2 per cent per year, and in the opinion of experts the annual rate of output, especially in South Africa, which at present provides about half of the total, is likely to decline. We may therefore have to settle down to a rate of increase in the world's stock of not much over 1 per cent per year, or just about enough to balance the rate of increase in the world's population. If therefore we are content to keep the price of *labour* from falling, this should content us: but if we wish to keep the price of *goods*, even of retail goods, from falling, we should perhaps require a rate of increase of something more like $2\frac{1}{2}$ or 3 per cent per year to balance the increase in individual productivity which may fairly be expected to occur in the years ahead.

At the same time we cannot be certain that the boot will not be on the other leg. If the technique of banking were to make great progress throughout the world, and if the spirit of amity and confidence between nations were to grow so firm that every country positively preferred to keep its reserves in its neighbours' pockets rather than its own, a universal gold standard could be made to work with a very sparing use of actual gold. Only in that case it would be exceedingly difficult to prevent a violent *fall* in the value of gold, and consequently of every monetary unit which is being kept equal to a defined weight of gold. Nor can we dismiss the possibility that the spread of education and the industrial revolution in India and the East generally may lead to a change in the habits of the Eastern peasant, who has hitherto tended to regard the wearing or burying of the precious metals as the only reputable form of saving—even to a vomiting forth of some of the vast supplies of gold which have been swallowed up for this purpose throughout the course of history.

In any case the very uncertainty of the future of the value of gold establishes the point. It is difficult to regard as very stable or sacred a standard of value which is liable to be upset by the discovery of new mines or processes of mining, by a decision on the part of some State to achieve the gold standard or of some other State to abandon it, by a sloughing off of the hereditary taboos of the Indian ryot or the London banker. The value of a yellow metal, originally chosen as money because it tickled the fancy of savages, is clearly a chancy and irrelevant thing on which to base the value of our money and the stability of our industrial system.[1]

[1] Cf. Keynes, *Indian Currency and Finance*, p. 101.

§ **4. The Case for Conformity to a World Gold Standard.**
Cannot we then devise a better way? Having made so much
progress in the manipulation of token money cannot we make
a little more? We could not abolish banking and note-issuing
even if we wished to: cannot we learn to control them on a
scientific basis? It is no wonder that not only 'needs of
trade' enthusiasts but sober and academic philosophers should
cry out against the artificiality and irrelevance of the gold
standard, and propose that for attaining our object, whatever
precisely it may be, we should rely wholly, and not as we do at
present only partially, on the conscious and deliberate regulation of the supply of money. The strength of the case for
adopting this proposal in any particular country depends partly
on whether the rest of the world is or is not on a gold standard.
For if it is, against the defects of the gold standard must be
set the undoubted convenience of maintaining stable rates of
exchange with the rest of the world. The importance of this
consideration of course varies with the size of the part played
by foreign trade in the economic life of the country concerned.
It is arguable, for instance, that India, when she drifted off the
gold standard in the days of the Great Muddle, suffered little
from the instability of the foreign exchanges compared with
what she gained by being able to keep her internal price-level
far more stable than would have been possible if the fortunes
of her money had remained tied to those of the English pound
or even of gold. But Great Britain is more dependent than
most countries on buying abroad foodstuffs and raw materials,
which have to be paid for in foreign money, and on selling
abroad the products of her industry, for which payment has
to be accepted in foreign money. To her, therefore, stability
of the exchanges is a peculiar convenience. Further, as a
result partly of her early adoption and long operation of a
gold standard, she has built up a big business as a provider of
financial machinery for the conduct of the world's foreign
trade, and as a clearing-house for the international borrowing
and lending of capital. This financial leadership of London
is a source of direct profit to a few, and also of indirect benefit

to many, because London's right to demand payment from foreigners for its services strengthens the lien which the whole country holds on the food products and raw materials of the world. Here then are strong reasons for doing as our neighbours do—though not perhaps so overwhelmingly strong as they are sometimes represented by interested parties. For there are ways, as experience showed, of minimising the inconveniences of fluctuating exchanges; and as for the financial leadership of London—well, there is some little danger that the strong vested interests thus created, by attributing to the gold standard, in season and out of season, not only the virtues which it possesses but also others in which it is singularly deficient, may delay unduly the day in which the world is ready for a more reasonable way of doing business.

§ 5. The General Case for the Gold Standard.   Why then has the world at large not yet shown itself ready for such a step? Perhaps in this as in so many other respects the year 1919 was the year of lost opportunities.   Perhaps in those heroic days, when men's mind were impressed with the strangeness of the situation in which they found themselves and of the chances which it offered for the building of a new world, it might have been possible to take this definite step along with others towards acquiring control of the material forces before which humanity suffers itself to be driven as before the wind.   But with every month that passed it became more difficult.   Baffled and bewildered and disillusioned with the new world, the business community has sought increasingly to recapture the comparative stability and peace of the world before the war. Nor can we dismiss its behaviour as mere blind and unreasoning conservatism.   We must remember the enormous impetus to which any banking system is subject, both from within and without, towards increasing continually the volume of its loans, and the formidable difficulty of so regulating the supply of money as really to meet the legitimate needs of trade.   We must remember, too, the pressure exerted upon Governments in the name of the consumer to provide this and that—coal or railway-transport or house-room—by some means or other below its economic cost. It is not surprising if both bankers and Governments in their more responsible moments desire to have some charm more potent than a mere metaphysical index-number both to elevate before the people and to contemplate in the privacy of their own cells. There are the same arguments against disturbing the simple faith of the banker and the City journalist (the politician perhaps has none) as against disturbing that of the pious savage. If a gold standard had never existed, it might be necessary to invent something of the kind for their benefit.

It is said that there was once a mine manager in Johannesburg who had a glass eye. When business called him away he would take his eye out and leave it in a prominent place; and while the master's eye was on them the workmen continued to work like blacks, as indeed they were. But one day one of the workmen, more daring than the rest, stealthily approached the all-seeing orb and covered it up with an inverted cigarette tin: whereupon he and all his fellows promptly went away and got drunk. Which is a parable of what might happen if all semblance of a gold standard were obliterated.

Here is another parable which has, apparently, the merit of being true.[1] There is among the Caroline Islands an island called Uap, whose money consists solely of huge stones called *fei*, many of them so large that they cannot be moved, so that even when they change hands in the course of business their physical location is left unchanged. In fact, the richest family in the island holds that position in virtue of being the owner of a huge stone, which was accidentally sunk from a raft while it was being brought to the island many years ago. For several generations this stone has been lying at the bottom of the sea, and none of the present generation of the family has ever seen it; but nobody questions that they are the richest family in the island. Some time ago the natives allowed the roads of the island to fall into disrepair, and steadily refused

[1] Furness, *Island of Stone Money*, Chap. VII, quoted in *Economic Journal*, June 1915, p. 281.

to mend them; and the Germans, who were at that time in possession of the island, had to devise some means of inflicting a fine. It was clearly useless to attempt to remove any of the stones from the island. 'At last,' so the account runs, 'by a happy thought the fine was exacted by sending a man to every *failu* and *pabai* throughout the disobedient districts, where he simply marked a certain number of the most valuable *fei* with a cross in black paint to show that the stones were claimed by the Government. This instantly worked like a charm; the people, thus dolefully impoverished, turned to and repaired the highways to such good effect from one end of the island to the other that they are now like park drives. Then the Government despatched its agents and erased the crosses. Presto! the fine was paid, the happy *failus* resumed possession of their capital stock, and rolled in wealth.' Just so gold is a fetish, if you will, but it does the trick.

§ 6. The Control of the World Value of Gold.

But if we decide to acquiesce silently for the present in the maintenance of a gold standard by the world, and in the adhesion to that standard of our own country, may we not at least hope that the monetary authorities of the world will do their best, by collective action, to prevent the misbehaviour of gold? That hope first dawned on mankind at a conference of experts held at Genoa in 1922; and it received strong nourishment in the ensuing years from the American experiment (p. 67) in the art of making use of gold as a handy person to have about the house, and a good influence on the whole on its inmates, without submitting to his tyrannical dictation. The essence of this experiment consists, it will be remembered, in enfeebling the link which binds the supply of bank money to the supply of gold, by varying the proportion which the Central Bank keeps between its reserves and its deposits. Of the mechanism by which this is effected it will be more convenient to speak later in another connection (Chapter VIII, § 2): at present it is enough to grasp the general idea of the control of the world value of gold.

The men of Genoa, more imaginative than the men of Brussels (p. 103), recommended that the Bank of England should summon a conference of the Central Banks of the world to explore ways and means of achieving this end. Up till 1928 no such conference had been called: but it would be unfair to assume that the matter has not occupied the thoughts of the responsible authorities, including those of that silent Sphinx, the Bank of England. Those scurryings of important financial persons across the Atlantic of which we read from time to time in our daily papers must surely have been concerned in part at least with this vital matter. Nevertheless it is difficult at present to feel confident that the policy is being pursued with sufficient vigour to ensure its triumph over all the perils described in § 3. A determined bout of gold-hoggery by a few free and independent nations might be very difficult to counter: a sudden rheum of the world's gold-glands might call for an alarmingly intricate and expensive operation of sterilisation. If gold is really to become a Merovingian monarch, with the central bankers of the leading countries as joint Mayors of the Palace, a good many of the objections which have been urged against the gold standard (as well as a good many of the arguments which have been used in its favour) fall to the ground. But if his tutelage is successfully enforced he may become in time such a figure of fun that he is laughed into surrendering even his titular crown. On the other hand the time may come when he attempts such a bold and disastrous *coup d'état* for the recovery of his lost powers that he is dragged at last to the scaffold amidst universal execration.

7. The Case for Re-valuation of the Pound. There is yet one more question for Englishmen to face in connection with this matter of the standard. Granted that we are right to retain a gold standard, are we also right to retain the figure of 113 grains laid down in 1816 and again in 1925 as the weight of fine gold to the value of which the value of the pound sterling is to be kept equal? There are perhaps few people who feel any doubt about the answer; yet it is by no means self-evident. For if it be true that by the Act of 1925 a stone was tied round the neck of the export trades (p. 109), and if it be true that the political and psychological obstacles to the removal of that stone by the contraction of the money-supply have hitherto proved irresistible (p. 110), and if it be true that the world value of gold is more likely to rise than to fall (p. 118), then the prescription of a lower value for the pound in terms of gold might well prove the simplest way of closing the gap between the internal and external price-levels, and of finding a way at last (p. 102) into the promised garden. True, we should have to expect some rise in the price of imports, and therefore in the cost of living for everybody: but would not that be the least painful way of restoring the balance between those of us who are sheltered from the blows of foreign competition and those luckless persons who, whether making for home or foreign markets, are exposed to their full force? The 'sound money' men may throw up their hands at the very idea of what they would regard as a gross breach of contract, and as a surrender of ground so painfully won. But others, whose daily life takes them oftener among factories and mean streets than into the parlours of the City of London, will not be able to shut their ears to the tramping of a million unemployed men. They will not only recall how unemployment breaks the lives and spirits of those that suffer it: they will appeal also to the great and growing volume of conviction that its spectre is the source of perhaps one-half of the disgruntlement of those who remain at work. Restriction of output, restriction of entry, restriction of inventive power, restriction of human kindliness and decent feeling—these are the acknowledged offspring of that terrible figure with the folded hands. What, we may well ask, is the worth of financial respectability won at such a cost?

And if it comes to contracts—well, contracts in England are made in terms of pounds sterling and not of lumps of gold. Moreover, there is one contract to which we are all parties, and out of which we have been allowed to do very badly—

namely, the payment of interest to our fellow-citizens on some £6000 million of National Debt, and the gradual repayment of the principal. The real burden of this debt has been increased by something like one-third by the rise in the value of money since it was incurred[1]: and our creditors could scarcely regard themselves as very badly treated if they were asked to surrender a little of this windfall gain, and debarred from obtaining that further windfall which would accrue to them from our following the alternative policy of beating down still further the level of internal prices.

§ 8. The Case Against the Re-valuation of the Pound.

Once we compel ourselves to approach the matter with an open mind, these arguments are seen to possess very great force. But we must pause a moment before being carried away by them to the point of action. In the first place, we must be sure of our facts. It may be true that, converted at the current rates of exchange, the level of internal prices and of money wages is higher in England than in some other countries with which her manufacturers and farmers are in active competition. But that has always been true, even in the palmiest days of the gold standard. If one country is superior to another in natural resources, in capital equipment, in the personal efficiency of its managers and its workpeople, or if it has more legal claims on the rest of the world or fewer obligations to discharge, then an hour's labour in the first country will command more gold than an hour's labour in the second; and this will be reflected directly in a higher level of money wages and indirectly, under some conditions, in a higher level of internal prices.[2] The fact therefore that money wages and internal prices are now lower in France or Belgium than in England may not be due to more than a small extent to the aftermath of stabilisation (p. 110), or imply any very unfair or

[1] Keynes, *Economic Journal*, June 1927, p. 212.

[2] Under independent standards, such sources of superiority will be reflected in a more favourable rate of exchange with the second country than would otherwise prevail. See note, p. 60.

abnormal handicap on the English manufacturer: it may be for the most part simply a sign that Frenchmen and Belgians in general are in a worse position than Englishmen in general for securing a handsome share of the world's good things.   If these differences in money wages are exactly compensated for by differences in the personal efficiency of the workpeople, the English manufacturer whose products are in competition with French or Belgian products will have nothing whatever to complain of: but if they are not, things may be very awkward for him.   From the point of view of the whole country however the ideal solution in the long run would be not to make things easier for the harassed exporter, but to change the character, and perhaps to diminish the volume, of its foreign trade.   Now there are good reasons for thinking that the difficulties of many of our leading export trades (in particular coal and cotton) are due not wholly or mainly to the after-effects of monetary disorder, but to much more deep-seated and intractable causes.   If the results of these difficulties are very grave, and if their removal necessitates a long and difficult process of reorganisation, it may be our duty to assuage the pain, if we are able, by monetary tinkerings: but we must not flatter ourselves that we are touching the heart of the trouble, and we may be doing something to delay its radical cure.

Secondly, we must remember that there is nothing good nor bad but thinking makes it so.   Against the proposed re-valuation of the pound is arrayed all the instinctive horror of a 'debasement of the coinage' inbred in the posterity of the subjects of Angevin and Tudor monarchs.   It may be slightly ludicrous that creditors (not to mention the owners of house-property and of railways) who accepted with nothing worse than a grumble the halving of their incomes in terms of goods, should be up in arms at the mention of a reduction of 10 per cent in their income in terms of gold, which scarcely one of them ever wishes to buy.   But if they feel like that, and if the high priests of finance sympathise with those feelings and are prepared to sabotage any measure which flouts them, there

10

are solid reasons of expediency against pressing on with such a measure unless the need is overwhelming and the benefits to be gained clear. In the judgment of the present writer, conditions might arise in which it would be imperative to take the bull by the horns and to remind our creditor classes that their contracts are in terms of pounds sterling and not of gold: but in this autumn of 1928 he is not prepared to plump boldly for such a course.

CHAPTER VIII

THE QUESTION OF THE CYCLE

The chief difficulty Alice found at first was with her flamingo:
... generally, just as she had got its neck straightened out, and
was going to give the hedgehog a blow with its head, it *would*
twist itself round and look up in her face.

Alice's Adventures in Wonderland

§ 1. Money in a Trade Boom. In this last chapter let us take
it for granted that England and most other important countries
remain on a gold standard, and refrain from revaluing their
moneys in terms of gold; and also that by concerted action the
Central Banks have brought the value of gold sufficiently under
control to protect it both from violent spasms due to isolated
acts of gold-hoggery and from long sweeping movements due
to gradual changes in the conditions of supply and in human
habits. Does there then remain anything for monetary policy
to accomplish? Yes. For history teaches us that besides the
long sweeping movements mentioned above there have frequently occurred also swinging changes in the value of money,
relatively short in duration but fairly ample in size—influenced
in their course by the longer sweeps, but apparently different
from them in nature and not explicable in the same terms.

These swings in the value of money are bound up with
roughly similar swings in output, employment, and consumption (not to mention such things as births and bankruptcies),
and if we try to analyse them we very soon get heavily involved
in our old troubles about what is cause and what is effect.
Many fat books have been written on the subject, and we are
still a long way from understanding it completely. It is not
even clear whether the old-fashioned European 'trade cycle'

which we used to know, with a swing of from seven to ten years, is going to exist at all in the future: America, in this as in other matters, has speeded things up, and seems to prefer a 'business cycle' of two or three years' duration or even less. It is obviously impossible in the closing pages of this little book to plunge deeply into these difficult matters: but it is equally impossible to evade them altogether. For the truth seems to be that the element of play in the gold standard has been used in the past to aggravate these cyclical movements: and the question naturally arises whether it cannot and should not be used rather to restrain them.

Let us suppose that for any reason (say to take advantage of a new invention, or a new method of industrial organisation, or the openings for development in a new country, or perhaps just out of sheer restlessness[1] and lightness of heart), those in control of industry decide to speed up the rate of growth of their output. It is easy to see that as a preliminary measure there will be needed a speeding-up in the rate of growth of their circulating capital (p. 85). To effect this they will come to the banks for help: and in default of other immediately available sources of additional saving they are likely even to increase the *proportion* of their total requirements for which they rely on the aid of the banks (p. 88). Thus a pressure is set up on the banks; and the banks, so far as they allow themselves to submit to it, pass it on to the public in the form of rising prices and enforced saving (p. 75). And once the rise in prices sets in, there are all sorts of reasons why it should tend to continue and to grow in strength. Those peculiarities in the forces determining the value of money which we found at work in periods of monetary collapse (p. 98) are to be found at work also, though in milder form, in periods of trade boom. The velocity of circulation of money increases: expecting prices to rise still further, the manufacturer presses on with his orders for raw materials, the retailer lays in stocks of finished goods, and even the thoughtful consumer hurries on with the purchase

[1] Schumpeter, 'The Explanation of the Business Cycle,' *Economica*, December, 1927.

of a new motor-car or a new suit of clothes. The university don and the widow, hit by the rise in prices, wonder whether it is really sensible to keep so large a balance at the bank. Thus the willingness of the public to perform saving in monetary form is sapped and undermined as a result of the very fact that additional calls have been made upon it.

And if the expansion in the supply of money thus undermines the demand, the decline in the demand stimulates the expansion of the supply (p. 98). The transaction-value of money is divorced from its income-value: goods at wholesale change hands at prices depending on the *expected* level of retail prices at a later date. And even for goods at wholesale prices are asked and offered which are justified not by the existing supply of money but by what it is expected to become by the time delivery is made. Apart altogether from increasing his real commitments, the merchant finds that he needs more money to carry the same volume of goods that he used to carry, the manufacturer that he needs more money to buy his usual supplies of materials and pay his usual labour-force. And of course both of them come trotting round to the bank. Thus to the bankers their ever-expanding volume of loans appears as a *result* and not as a *cause* of the rise in prices: while we, sitting up in the clouds, can see that the confident expectation that they *would* expand their loans was the essential condition for the occurrence of so great a rise, and that if they were to act otherwise than is expected of them the rise could not be sustained.

Nor is this all. The piling-up of stocks in the hands of merchants and retailers involves a lengthening of the total period of production of goods (p. 85): and as the rate of output approaches the limit of what, with the existing plant and labour force, it is physically possible to produce, that period is still further lengthened by delays and congestions of all kinds arising within the actual processes of manufacture and transport. Thus the requirements of the business world for circulating capital are still further increased, and the pressure on the banks reinforced.

The compliance of the banking system reaches its limits when it becomes seriously concerned about its reserves: but long before that point is reached there is time for much damage to be done. We shall be wise indeed to suspend judgment as to whether industrial progress as we know it can be expected to continue at an absolutely even pace, and without *any* variation in the calls which are made on the public through the banking system for the provision of saving. But we need feel no doubt that if these variations must occur, their secondary consequences ought to be kept strictly in control. The dissipation of savings which have been embodied in monetary form, the artificial lengthening of the period of production by what our ancestors called the forestalling and engrossing of goods, the numerous errors of judgment and forecast which mark the course of a trade boom—these things are evils in themselves and bring evils more spectacular in their train. We have a right to ask that our monetary system should be so managed as to restrain and not to promote them.

§ **2. The Mechanism of Control by the Central Bank.** What weapons are available for this purpose? So far as the trouble is due to the mere magnitude of the loans being extended by the banks, and so far as these banks are adhering rigidly to their rules about reserves, it would seem that the evil can be held in check if the Central Bank can succeed in restricting the growth of the chequeries kept with itself by the ordinary banks. Thus the weapon at its disposal for countering the misbehaviour of gold (p. 123) is at its disposal also for countering a misbehaviour in the value of money for which the blame cannot be laid upon that convenient whipping-boy: and it is time now to disclose more precisely what that weapon is. It is a double-headed axe, and its first blade consists in the sale to the public of Government securities. For if the Bank of England sells £1000 of War Loan to John Smith, John Smith will pay the Bank of England with a cheque on (say) Barclays, and the Bank of England will therefore be able to dock Barclays' chequery with itself by £1000. But this will upset Barclays' proportion between its reserves and its deposits, and to restore that proportion it will be obliged to cut down its loans. Thus by a reverse process to that described on page 93, the sale of £1000 of War Loan by the Bank of England enforces a reduction of the aggregate bank deposits of the country by about nine times that amount.

This is a very powerful blade, and its use has been reduced to a fine art, both in England and in America, in recent years. But it may not on all occasions be sharp enough to do the trick. For it is the practice in America that an ordinary bank may borrow from its Reserve Bank (p. 47): and it is the custom in England that certain classes of borrowers, namely, those who are concerned with the financing of foreign trade, may rely at a pinch on borrowing from the Bank of England. Thus if an American bank finds its reserves cut down in this way, it will be able to replenish them by borrowing from its Reserve Bank: while if an English bank is placed in a similar position, some of the borrowers whom it turns away will be able to persuade the Bank of England to create chequeries for them; and the cheques drawn on these chequeries will be paid into the ordinary banks, which will thus find their chequeries at the Bank of England augmented once more.

To protect itself against these assaults, the Central Bank is obliged on occasion to bring into play the other head of its axe. It raises the rate of interest at which it will lend—in America to the other banks, in England to those who are engaged in financing foreign trade. In England this raising of the Bank rate, by choking off borrowers from the Bank of England, pretty effectively prevents the banks' chequeries at the Bank of England from being replenished by the process just described. In America this result is perhaps less certainly to be counted on. It may indeed be argued that *some* transactions which, having regard to the trouble and risk involved, were just profitable to the banks when they could borrow from their Reserve Bank at a certain rate of interest, will cease to be profitable if they can only borrow at a higher rate: thus their eagerness to borrow will be diminished, and the decision of the

Reserve Bank to curtail their chequeries will be at all events partially carried into effect. In so far, however, as an *individual* bank can do what the banking system *as a whole* undoubtedly does—namely, expand its loans by an amount considerably greater than an accession to its reserves—the force of this argument is seriously weakened.[1]

Experience shows that if the rise in the rate of interest demanded by the Central Bank is sufficiently pronounced, it will be followed by a rise in the rates demanded by the other banks as well. Exactly why this should happen it is not very easy to explain. In America it is possible to argue, somewhat on the lines of the last paragraph, that if the banks must pay more for what they borrow they must naturally charge more for what they lend; but there is the same weak spot in the argument. And for England, where the banks are not borrowers from the Bank of England, this explanation clearly will not serve; and the chief proximate cause impelling them to raise their rates seems to be the force of long-established custom— the knowledge that that is the course of action expected of them by the Bank of England, and an implicit confidence that the Bank of England does not act without good reason. And perhaps in America also the most important connecting-link is a psychological one of this kind.

If we must be careful in phrasing our account of the cause of the rise in general interest rates, so must we also in phrasing our account of its effect in contracting the supply of money. There is no need to dispute the common view—that by directly deterring a number of borrowers from applying for aid to the banks, it facilitates the task of the latter in cutting down their loans and therefore their deposits. But in England, at all events, in view of the observed constancy of the proportion maintained by the banks between their reserves and their deposits, we cannot well regard the rise in interest rates as more than a convenient mechanism for enforcing a decision about the magnitude of their deposits at which they have arrived on

[1] J. S. Lawrence, 'Borrowed Reserves and Bank Expansion,' *Quarterly Journal of Economics*, August, 1928.

other grounds—namely, the size of their reserves.   In America it is a little different: if the reserves of the banks are partly borrowed from their Reserve Bank, it is not impossible that in the casual sequence of events the high interest rates should come first, the decline in loans and deposits second, and the repayment of loans to the Reserve Bank, with a consequent shrinking in the ordinary banks' reserves, third.   In this event, the rise in general interest rates can be regarded as a semi-independent auxiliary to the restrictive action of the Central Bank—a third head, as it were, to the axe.   But in the main it seems better to regard it as an expedient adopted by the banks to aid them in carrying out the restrictive action forced upon them by the other two blades—the sale of securities and the raising of Central Bank rate; and to suspect that in so far as in America these other two blades are blunted by the power of the banks to borrow reserves, this third blade cannot be relied upon to render much assistance.

But on these difficult matters the reader may well be excused from seeking further enlightenment in this little book, and the author from trying to impart it.   It is enough to realise that by the use of their double weapon, Central Banks can up to a point check the expansion of the money-supply; and that while we cannot be sure that their power to do so is in all circumstances complete,   there is good reason to believe that if it were used earlier and more resolutely than it has sometimes been in the past, many of the evil excrescences of a trade boom could be lopped away.

§ **3. The Stimulation of Saving.**   A rise in general interest rates is apt to exercise two other effects on the course of a trade boom, of which the one may be embarrassing and the other helpful to the policy of the Central Bank.   Both of them arise out of the fact that the rise is not confined to the rates at which the banks will lend, but extends also to those which they allow to their depositors.   In England, it is true, many people do not succeed in getting any interest at all on their current accounts; but deposit accounts which can be drawn against at seven days' notice earn a rate of interest which is fixed by agreement between the banks at 2 per cent below Bank rate, and therefore rises when Bank rate rises. And deposits which require longer notice of withdrawal are allowed higher rates of interest than this, especially if they are owned by foreigners.

Now if interest rates rise in England (say) as compared with France, England becomes a good country in which to lend and a bad country in which to borrow. Frenchmen will become anxious to obtain English money, and those Frenchmen who have it will be unwilling to part with it. Moreover certain Englishmen who want to borrow money, instead of borrowing it in England, will borrow it in France, and will sell the claims to French money thus obtained for English money with which to conduct their business. Thus the rate of exchange will turn against France and in favour of England: and under a gold standard this may go so far that it becomes cheaper to send gold to England from France than to buy claims to English money.

This attraction of gold from abroad has indeed been in the past the main motive impelling Central Banks to raise their rate of interest in the later phases of a trade boom. For the additional money created during the boom gives the people of the country an increased command over the goods which are the subject of international trade, stimulates imports and checks exports, and turns the exchanges against the country, leading ultimately to an outflow of gold. The raising of the rate of interest thus presents itself to the Central Bank as a corrective measure, designed to restore the *status quo*, and as such fulfils its limited purpose well enough. But we are now forcing ourselves to visualise a state of affairs in which the Central Bank intervenes much earlier in the boom to prevent its extravagances from developing; and in this case the incidental result of a rise in interest-rates in attracting foreign gold may be a positive hindrance to the Central Bank in carrying out the task to which it has set its hand. For the result of the import of gold will be to increase the chequeries of the banks just when the Central Bank is trying to curtail them, and so to necessitate still greater efforts at curtailment on its part.

This consideration, so far as it goes, tells against the use of the blade of interest-rates so long as the blade of security-sales can be made to serve.

The rise in deposit-rates has also however a less objectionable effect. It tempts depositors in general to moderate the velocity with which they permit their chequeries to circulate. Those who have money on current account may be induced to transfer it to deposit account: those who have money on deposit account may be dissuaded from using it to buy shares in industrial companies who would have kept it, or paid it away to others who would have kept it, on current account. To the bankers themselves it may even seem that it is their offer of high rates that is increasing the sum total of their deposits. We know better (p. 78) than to suppose that this can be true: but we also know that such action by depositors increases the real saving which they are voluntarily putting at the disposal of industry through the medium of the banks. If, therefore, it does not help to extinguish the flames of the trade boom, it at least—unlike the import of gold—provides a modicum of *genuine* fuel wherewith they can be stoked without accentuating the rise in prices: and we should be rash to turn up our noses at such an offering.

In this connection it will be convenient to examine the results of another action which experience shows that the banks are likely to take in a time of trade boom. Finding the making of loans profitable, they are likely to sell some of their Government securities to the public, and to expand their loans instead. Since the public's chequeries are reduced by the purchase of the investments by just so much as they are augmented by the expenditure of the proceeds of the loans, the transaction involves no net change in the magnitude of the banks' deposits. Whether or not it dispenses with the need for the rise in prices which would otherwise follow from the making of additional loans depends on whether the public, in buying the securities, was performing an additional act of saving, or whether it was merely substituting saving embodied in the form of Government securities for saving embodied in the form of chequeries.

If the latter only, then this transaction, like the import of gold, is only a device for assisting the banks to impose enforced saving on the public without getting into trouble about their proportion of reserves to deposits. But if the former, then by increasing the proportion of resources under their control which is embodied in circulating capital, the banks will have done something to compensate for the increase in the proportion of circulating capital which has to be provided with their aid (see Ch. V, § 8, and App. B).

§ 4. The Qualitative Control of Bank Loans. The methods of control hitherto discussed call for the exercise of initiative and public spirit by the Central Bank only; nothing is asked of the ordinary banks save to follow the dictates of enlightened self-interest, tempered by customary loyalties and taboos. It seems to be the general opinion that this is all that need be asked; and further that in the existing state of the world, and especially where, as in America, the banks are numerous, small and scattered, it is all that it is any use asking. Yet a case can be made out for the opposite view, and for holding that in England at all events, where the banks are great semi-public corporations with large powers and a high sense of responsibility, they might fairly and profitably be asked to co-operate more actively in the policy of damping down the trade boom by having careful regard to the *quality* as well as the *quantity* of their lending operations.

An attempt has indeed been made in America, and in some other countries whose legislation has been modelled on hers, to bring this matter also partly within the province of the Central Bank. An American bank borrowing from its Reserve Bank has in effect to give as pledge for the loan either Government securities or rapidly maturing obligations of business men which represent actual goods at some stage in the process of production; and paper of this latter kind must be held by the Reserve Banks themselves against such part of their note-issue as is not covered by gold. The intention of these provisions was to ensure that loans created with the aid of the Reserve Banks should be used solely for the provision of circulating capital: and it was even claimed that so long as this intention was realised, the system could not be guilty of an excessive creation of money.[1]   Of the theoretical weakness of the 'needs of trade' theory, which in this legislation finds its most distinguished expression, enough has been said in Chapter V: the point which concerns us now is that the intention of the law was never realised.   Apart from the incongruity of admitting Government securities on the same footing as genuine 'commercial paper,' experience has shown that it is easy for the banks to borrow from their Reserve Bank in the prescribed manner, and on the strength of the reserves thus acquired to expand by a much greater amount their investments in industrial securities or their loans to operators on the stock exchange: and it is now generally admitted that the Reserve Banks can exert little influence over the method of employment, as distinct from the total amount, of the loanable funds of the ordinary banks.[2]

In England it is still more obvious that if qualitative discrimination between the uses of money is desirable, it is to the ordinary banks that we must look for its exercise.   Now of course to some extent such discrimination is always being practised.   No doubt the bankers exercise a kind of selective preference in favour of those borrowers in whose probity, competence and business prospects they feel a particular confidence.   No doubt, too, as one of their leaders has told us,[3] the six months or seasonal loan is still the backbone of their business; and their desire that their loans shall be fairly regularly and frequently paid off must work in the same direction as a rule that their resources shall be employed for preference in the building up of circulating capital.   Nevertheless there are two features of English banking practice which from our present standpoint seem to require rather careful scrutiny.

[1] *Report of the Federal Reserve Board for 1923*, p. 34.
[2] Burgess, *The Reserve Banks and the Money Market*, p. 179.
[3] Leaf, *Banking*, p. 164.

The first is the fact already noted (p. 93) that in many cases —how large a proportion of cases we are not allowed to know —the banker's main concern seems to be to have tangible evidence that the borrower is a man of substance, in the form of some piece of property or stock exchange security which he can sell up if the borrower fails to repay him, and the nature of which has no necessary bearing whatever on the enterprise in which the borrower is engaged.   This plan has its advantages, first in ensuring that money does not get into the hands of mere adventurers and 'men of straw,' and secondly in preventing anything like that 'tied house' system—that intricate interweaving of banking and industrial interests—which has gone far in some countries to bring the whole of industry under financial domination.   But from our present standpoint of control of the trade cycle it obviously has its disadvantages as well; for it means that the banker regards it as outside his province to enquire too closely into the uses to which his loan is being put, or to consider their bearing on the value of money and the stability of trade.

§ 5. The Manipulation of the Rate of Interest.   The second practice of the English bankers which requires scrutiny is the large measure of reliance which they place on a rise in the rate of interest as a sieve for thinning out the stream of demand for loans.   As already stated (p. 134) we must not exaggerate the importance of this instrument: for it would be little short of a miracle if it proved adequate by itself to reduce the stream to precisely that volume which week by week, having regard to the size of their reserves, the bankers are prepared to satisfy.   Yet there seems no reason to doubt that they look to it for assistance in their task: and there is one general and two rather special arguments which can be put forward in favour of their doing so.   The general argument is that this method tends to leave the ultimate disposal of the available resources in the hands of the business world.   The banks decide what total sum shall be lent, the business world decides how that sum shall be used; and the business world being a complex of specialists and experts in particular lines, while the banks are mere general practitioners, there is some reason for thinking that its judgment as to the directions in which the community's limited resources can be most fruitfully applied will be superior to theirs. A rise in the rate of interest charged by the banks chokes off those borrowers who do not feel confident that the public's demand for the product in which they are interested will justify their paying the higher rate: and this in the main is as it should be.

The special arguments refer to two classes of loan which are specially responsible, in times of trade boom, for sowing the seeds of future trouble, and for checking which a rise in the rate of interest seems at first sight a peculiarly appropriate instrument. The first consists in loans to those 'speculators' who when prices are rising buy goods merely for the purpose of selling them again at enhanced prices. Now the ethics and economics of speculation in general lie outside the subject-matter of this book. It must suffice here to say that speculation in some commodity of which there is likely to be a future shortage renders at any rate an incidental service to the community; but the kind of speculative activity which characterised the winter of 1919–20—a wild speculation in commodities in general and even in the instruments of production such as cotton-mills, a speculation born of rising prices and expanding bank loans—serves no useful end, and is a chief begetter of the industrial depression which inevitably follows. Now by raising the price which speculators must pay for the where-withal to carry their stocks of goods, bankers can reduce the profitableness, and so curtail the volume, of transactions of this kind.[1]

The second class of loans which especially needs watching in times of trade boom is in its nature more commendable, but in its consequences sometimes hardly less disastrous. It consists in loans which are employed in the construction of fixed capital, whether for retention by the owner (as when a cotton-spinner enlarges his factory) or for sale in the market (as when a

[1] Cf. Mr. McKenna, speech of January 28, 1921.

ship-builder builds a ship). Such loans do not, even when they have fulfilled their purpose, bring on to the market an immediate flow of *consumable* goods: and their effect therefore in imposing enforced saving on the consuming public is peculiarly severe. Further, it is in this field that the danger of miscalculations and errors of judgment is most acute. Now in enterprises of this kind, which take a long time in coming to fruition, the rate of interest is a specially important consideration. This is easy to see when the capital instrument remains in the possession of the owner, and he continues to pay interest to the bank on the loan employed in its construction; but it is true also when it is sold for cash to a third party. For the price which such an instrument can be expected to fetch depends partly on the rate of interest which the potential buyer could obtain by investing his money in other ways. A rise in the general rate of interest lowers this price, and thus discourages the production of such instruments for sale. Thus by one route and another a rise in the rate of interest will have some effect in diverting the community's ready resources into avenues where they replace themselves more quickly, and will tend to restrain society from investing for a distant return more than it can really at the moment afford.[1]

§ 6. The Rationing of Bank Loans.
Here are strong arguments for relying heavily on variations in the rate of interest for regulating the volume of bank loans; but before accepting them as conclusive we must look a little further.

First, it does not seem likely that such variations can ever be completely effective for either of the two special purposes just discussed, unless indeed they are made so large as to be intolerable to the bulk of the ordinary non-speculative business community. When once the speculative spirit is abroad it is not so easily exorcised. The man who expects to make a money gain of 20 per cent by merely sitting for a few months on some bales of cotton or some barrels of oil will not be put off by a rise of 1 or 2 per cent *per annum* in the rate of interest

[1] Cf. Cassel, Memorandum for Brussels Conference, p. 23.

which he must pay to his bank. If the value of money is rapidly falling, a money rate of interest of even 10 per cent may represent a *real* rate of interest of less than nothing: for the £110 which he has to pay back to the bank may have less aggregate value than the £100 which he borrowed a year previously. Again, the future yields of constructional enterprise are at best difficult to forecast accurately or to bring into close comparison with present costs; and those who have made up their minds that what the world really requires is a Channel tunnel or an electrification of the railway system or a plant for harnessing the tides will not easily be persuaded otherwise. There are grounds, then, for suspecting that, in order to make their effect felt, moderate manipulations of the rate of interest may need at least to be supplemented by some kind of direct rationing of bank loans: and if the *quality* of bank loans outstanding were thus more effectively controlled, their *quantity* might no longer call for such rigorous restriction.

Secondly, the 'Trust the business man' argument needs perhaps the same kind of careful scrutiny as the 'Trust the man on the spot' argument in politics. The banker, seated at the heart of things, and not as a rule deeply entangled in any particular line of business, should be in some ways in a better position to form a dispassionate judgment on the relative prospects of different branches of industry than those whose business it is to hold that there is nothing like leather, or jute, or coffee, or whatever it may be. We must not underestimate the difficulty of the task set to the business world; but half a century of British shipping history (not to mention more recent happenings in the cotton and motor trades) forbids us to acclaim too enthusiastically the success with which it tackles it.

Thirdly, in the present temper of the world this argument must be reinforced by another. Production normally follows the behest only of those demands which can clothe and interpret themselves in terms of an offer of money. Now we may agree that this is an arrangement which it is neither possible nor desirable entirely to supplant (p. 4): but we may also reasonably hold that the communal mind is old enough and wise

11

enough to be allowed now and again to announce that there is some one thing which, whether or not it is a paying proposition, it will insist on having done. The present generation seems to have so made up its mind about the provision of working-class houses; and he must be a bold man who, knowing and visualising all the relevant social facts, declares that it is wrong. Now once such a decision has been deliberately taken it seems merely vexatious to hamper its execution by forcing the enterprise in question to submit to the ordeal by rate of interest. By that ordeal it would be rejected; but we know that already, and we have deliberately decided in this instance to go behind the test of money value. In such circumstances it may fairly be urged that the banks, being, when all is said and done, the servants of the community, should be instructed or exhorted or entreated to give effect to its wishes by putting a generous ration of loans at the disposal of the selected enterprise.

Finally, it is worth noting that the general arguments which tell against any attempt in normal times to control the price and ration the supplies of ordinary commodities appear to apply with considerably less force to the case of bank loans. The first is the danger of drying up the new supplies of any article which is sold for less than it might be made to fetch: the second is the inconvenience caused by tying customers down to a particular retailer, and the danger of evasion. The first argument is irrelevant to the case of bank loans, since the very object at which we are aiming is a partial drying up of the supply. The second argument loses much of its force, especially where, as in England to-day, the greater part of the business is in the hands of a few big and trustworthy banks. For people are much less likely to want to change their banker than their butcher; and we need not suppose any formal combination among the banks in order to feel pretty confident that they would succeed in detecting what the Americans call 'double borrowing,'[1] and in making tolerably effective any rationing policy with the spirit of which they were in broad agreement.

[1] Cf. Phillips, *Bank Credit*, pp. 302, 311–12.

It seems evident that in dealing with the monetary situation of 1920, the leaders of English banking—acting according to one of their number,[1] in complete independence of one another—applied these principles of selective rationing to a degree for which there was no precedent, and which would have scandalised some of their predecessors. Perhaps if they had applied it earlier and with more vigour and discretion, the shipyards and the cottonmills would be busier to-day. Whether the recognition of the need for such a change in banking practice would not insensibly impel the great banks toward closer union, and whether that again would not involve a greater measure of direct State control over the operations of banking, is another question which need not be pursued here.

§ 7. **The Need to Control Falling Prices.** Hitherto in this chapter we have been giving our whole mind to possible methods of controlling the upward swing of the trade cycle; and though at the time this book is published Englishmen may almost have forgotten what a trade boom looks like, we are right to give it the lion's share of our attention. For the common opinion that the more obvious evils of trade depression —bankruptcies, excessive contraction of output, unemployment and so forth—spring inevitably out of the preceding extravagances of the boom seems to be substantially correct: so that if we can prevent the latter we shall have prevented the former as well. Nevertheless we cannot be certain of being able to prevent the boom entirely, nor even, in the author's opinion, can we be certain that we want to. If it be true that industrial development, if we are determined to have it at all, must needs proceed to a certain extent by jerks, there will be times when a trans-continental railway has just been built which will meet all traffic needs for many years—when the street railway system of a country has been electrified or its merchant fleet converted to an oil basis—when every man, woman, and child possesses a motor-car—in short when a condition of temporary saturation with some important kind of equipment has been

[1] Mr. Walter Leaf, speech of February 3, 1921.

reached, and it is exceedingly difficult for mankind to switch his activities straight away on to the satisfaction of some new need. Under such conditions—and we should be rash to say we would rather they never occurred—the symptoms of industrial depression will develop. Further, there are other happenings which, though we can scarcely call them cyclical, are liable to produce scarcely distinguishable results. If private firms and joint-stock companies take to providing their circulating as well as their fixed capital largely out of their own reserves instead of having recourse to the banks—if the period of production is shortened by simplifying the types of goods produced and keeping smaller stocks of them on hand—if the public desires to propel a greater tide of saving through the channels of the banks, those who have fully grasped the importance of the four crucial fractions (Ch. V, § 8) will readily see that conditions are set up tending to a fall in prices and a wastage of saving. And Americans will perhaps not fail to recognise some features of their own recent history.

We must indeed remember the conclusion reached in Chapter VII, § 1, that it is not the *whole* of *every* fall in prices that we certainly desire to prevent. If productivity per head is rapidly increasing as a result of improvements in organisation and technique, we shall not necessarily accuse of inefficiency a monetary-system which fails to keep even retail prices, still less one which fails to keep wholesale prices, from falling. For such a fall will entail no direct leakage of saving (p. 81), and will have certain positively desirable results (p. 113): and while it will, like other falls, be damaging and discouraging to merchants and middlemen (which is perhaps one argument among many against our present excessive dependence on such persons), its discouraging effect on manufacturers themselves is easy to exaggerate. Unless we bear this important qualification in mind, we may run some risk of underestimating the success hitherto attained by the American banking system in its efforts at control (p. 67). At the same time we must admit that there are likely to be falls in prices which *are* wholly or partially damaging and which we *do* desire to check. It is important therefore for us to enquire what weapons are at the disposal of the monetary system for this purpose.

§ **8. Expedients for the Control of Falling Prices.**   Reflection shows that, whether we consider the Central Bank in relation to the other banks or the other banks in relation to the public, the available weapons are less efficient than those available for coping with a boom.   The Central Bank can, it is true, expand the chequeries of the ordinary banks by the converse of the method employed for curtailing them—namely, by the purchase of Government securities: but even this process may be gravely hampered where the banks are borrowers from the Central Bank, since by the repayment of loans they can, up to a point, deplete their chequeries as fast as they are being expanded as a result of the Central Bank's purchases of securities.   And as for the public, while by the method of rationing it is always possible to prevent their chequeries from exceeding any assigned amount, there is no counterpart to this method for forcing them to attain that amount.   Further, the rate of interest is a less effective auxiliary when prices are falling than when they are rising.   For supposing a man believes that the the £100 which he will have to pay back to the bank in a year's time will be worth 10 per cent more goods than the £100 which he borrows now, then he may well conclude that even if he were charged no interest at all the transaction would not be worth while.   And the bank has yet to be seen which will lend money for nothing or for a negative rate of money interest.

Thus the banking system may be hard put to it to make the money supply large enough, and keep it moving fast enough, to check the fall in prices.   But it will presumably be better placed for attaining this end if, as in America, it is itself ready to invest largely and boldly in industrial enterprises than if, as in England, it feels bound to keep its investments moderate in amount and predominantly 'gilt-edged' in character.   And per-haps nowadays, when a desire of the public to withdraw savings from the banking system takes the form rather of making their chequeries circulate faster (p. 79) than of clamouring for

common money, we ought to revise some of our old English
ideas about the undesirability of a bank taking action of this
kind.

There is one more expedient at the disposal of the banks—
an expedient, to the Victorian mind, of an even more dubious
kind. When you have pumped into the producer all the money
he can absorb, you can try it on the consumer as well. In
America in 1927 a sum of about £450 million, or about £4 per
head of the population, much of it provided by the banks, was
said to be outstanding on loans to consumers for the purchase
of motor-cars, saxophones and other desirable commodities.
There is much to be said about this system from other points of
view; from our present standpoint it appears as an ingenious
device for the preservation of stability in the value of money.

§ 9. The Scope for Government Intervention. Even so, however, it is, in the author's view, unlikely that the monetary
system will ever be able to cope unaided with a trade slump
(or phenomena akin to a trade slump) as efficiently as with a
trade boom (or phenomena akin to a trade boom). It is likely
to require the assistance of a more powerful ally—the Government of the country itself. What, after all, can be more
sensible than that the Central Government should organise a
collective demand for telephone equipment, or the local
governments a collective demand for municipal lavatories, to
take the place of an individual demand for ships or steel rails
which has rightly and reasonably fallen temporarily away?
If the public's desire to save is increasing so fast, or the processes of manufacture and salesmanship are being speeded up
so rapidly, that private industry is left bothered and bewildered
as to how to harness the productive forces thus released, what
can be more sensible that the Government, using the monetary
system as its handmaid, should intervene to turn them to good
account, instead of allowing them to leak away in the form of
unlooked-for windfalls to some and undeserved ruin to others?
Thus we are brought at last into contact with the high and
complex theme of the part proper to be played by Government

in the promotion and direction of economic progress.   But of that this much only can be said here.   Among the half-truths left us as a legacy by the Great Muddle is the doctrine that a banking system must at all costs be 'independent of the Government.'   If this means that a bank cannot be administered as if it were a tax-collector's office, or that a banker must not be pestered by daily questions in Parliament as to why he lent money to John Smith and not to William Brown, well and good.   But if it means that the monetary policy of a country should be carried on *in vacuo*, without reference to the problem of the development of the vast national estate, then it is a sterile and a dangerous doctrine indeed.

And so we are led back to where we began—the fact that money is a servant and not a master—a means and not an end. The real economic evils of society—inadequate production and inequitable distribution—lie too deep for any purely monetary ointment to cure.   An unwise monetary policy can wreak unmerited hardship and engender unnecessary confusion and waste: not even a wise one can turn a world which is unjust and poor into a world which is rich and just.   The mending of the road over which the produce passes to market is no substitute for the digging and dunging of the fields themselves.   No tinkering with counters will take us very far towards the discovery of an industrial system which shall supply both adequate incentives to those who venture and plan, and peace of mind to those who sweat and endure.

APPENDIX A

(I) CHAPTER II

Let R be   the real annual national income.

Let T be   the real annual volume of transactions.

Let M be   the quantity of money in existence.

Let K be   the proportion of R which people wish to have enough money on hand to purchase.

Let K′ be   the proportion of T which people wish to have enough money on hand to conduct.

Let V be   the average velocity of circulation of money against the constituents of real income.

Let V′ be   the average velocity of circulation of money against the constituents of real transactions.

Let P be   the income price-level.

Let P′ be   the transaction price-level.

Then we have   (i)   (a) $P = \dfrac{M}{KR}$

(b) $P' = \dfrac{M}{K'T}$

(ii)   (a) $P = \dfrac{MV}{R}$

(b) $P' = \dfrac{MV'}{T}$

APPENDIX A

(II) CHAPTER VI, § 4

A continuing increase in M will tend

- (1) to increase R and T, thereby checking the increase in P and P′,
- (2) to increase V and V′ (or diminish K and K′), thereby aggravating the increase in P and P′,
- (3) to increase V′ more than V (or diminish K′ more than K), and thereby increase P′ more than P.

In so far as present price-quotations refer to transactions to be closed at a future date, there is a further rise in P′, the cause of which can be represented in notation (i) by a further decrease of K′. But since the velocity of circulation of existing money is not increased to match, we must, in notation (ii), write

$$P' = \frac{(M + M')\ V'}{T}$$

where M′ is *latent* money not yet created.

There is also a further effect which for the sake of simplicity, since it does not affect P or P′, is not mentioned in the text. T increases out of proportion to R owing to an increase in the number of transactions in raw materials, capital goods, etc.: but this does no more than offset part (not the whole) of the increase in V′ as compared with V.

APPENDIX B

(I)   CHAPTER V, § 8

Let R be   the real annual national income.

Let K be   the proportion of this over which people wish to keep command in the form of money, so that KR is the aggregate real value of bank deposits.

Let C be   circulating capital.

Let D be   the proportion of a year which is covered by the period of production, so that DR is the real income during a period of production.

Let a be   the proportion of KR which the banks have crystallised in the form of circulating capital.

Let b be   the proportion of circulating capital which has been built up with the aid of the banks.

Then we have $a\mathrm{KR} = b\mathrm{C}$

$$\mathrm{C} = \tfrac{1}{2}\,\mathrm{DR}$$

$$\therefore\ a\mathrm{K} = \tfrac{1}{2}\,b\mathrm{D}$$

The greater is $\dfrac{\mathrm{D}}{\mathrm{K}}$ the greater must be $\dfrac{a}{b}$, i.e. given a, the smaller must be b, i.e. the less is the proportion of his circulating capital which the borrower can hope to raise through the bank without upsetting equilibrium.

APPENDIX B

(II) CHAPTER VIII

If b and D increase (§ 1), the imposition of forced saving can only be prevented if the banking system is able to make a corresponding increase in a and/or K (§ 3).

If K increases, while b and D diminish (§ 7), the banking system may be hard put to it, even if it can diminish a by increasing its investments, to prevent a fall in prices and a wastage of saving.

CHAPTER IX

MONEY IN THE SECOND GREAT MUDDLE

> Once more she found herself in the long hall, and close to
> the little glass table. 'Now I'll manage better this time,' she
> said to herself.
>
> *Alice's Adventures in Wonderland*

§ **1. The Great Slump.** 'We have now entered calmer waters.'
So the writer assured his readers in 1928 (p. 2); and so many,
with wiser heads than his, then hoped and believed. But about
a year later there set in the recession of trade which ushered in
the greatest slump in history and threw the world's monetary
arrangements once more into confusion. And when a partial
and uneasy stability had again been restored, there followed
the greatest war in history, and the monetary fat was in the fire
again. It is the story of money in this Second Great Muddle
—a muddle which is not yet cleared up—that this chapter
must, in brief and bare outline, attempt to tell. Attention is
directed to the fact that the typescript passed out of the writer's
hands early in 1947.

The fair-minded reader will admit that in the book which he
has just read he was given a few hints that everything in the
garden of 1928 was not perhaps so lovely as it looked: hints
that Europe was looking a bit wobbly on the stilts of the gold
exchange system (p. 118), and England a bit wobbly on the old
gold parity of the pound (pp. 110, 127): hints that even the
long golden age of American prosperity under the beneficent
sway (or such it seemed) of the Federal Reserve System had
some queer features about it (p. 146)—features which led
to its being described in retrospect as 'a sloom followed by a
bump.' But the writer makes no claim to have foreseen the

débâcle which followed, nor even to be clear now about the
relative strength of its various causes. This is one of the
episodes of history about which it is not very easy to be wise
even after the event.

Essentially, it would seem, what happened was not very
different from what had often happened before. There
occurred a condition of temporary saturation (p. 145) with
important kinds of capital equipment, notably in the United
States and in the countries which had been equipping or re-
equipping themselves with the aid of her savings. But this
occurred when certain awkward longer-run strains were already
making themselves felt. The first was the decline in the rate
of growth of population in the Western world—a change which
is apt to mean that the demand for staple necessaries does not
keep pace with the general growth of wealth, and hence that a
special nippiness and ingenuity is called for from those who
invest resources to supply the world's wants. The second was
the intensive application of scientific thought and method to the
arts of agriculture—a process full of promise for the future of
the world, but apt to lead to present ruin for those groups of
producers who are untouched by the new ways, and perhaps
even to an immediate decline of total income for those who
adopt them. So the agricultural populations of the world
were on the edge of trouble on their own account, and specially
prone to catch any infection which might reach them from the
industrial centres.

On the top of these general troubles were superimposed a
number of more particular ones. The war settlement had left
a network of public debts entailing an annual flow of funds
from poorer countries to richer ones—an arrangement calculated to work smoothly so long, but only so long, as the richer
countries would lend the money back to the poorer ones.
England was embarrassed by a weakness of exporting power
connected with the malaise of some of her leading industries
and her high level of industrial costs; and she was trying to
discharge the responsibilities laid upon her by the prevalence
of the gold exchange system (p. 64) without really being flush

enough of cash to do so. Finally, such is the American tem-
perament that the golden age culminated in an unprecedented
orgy of stock exchange speculation; and the Federal Reserve
authorities, hard put to it to know whether to nourish the
dying embers of the industrial boom or to pour water on the
stock market conflagration, have been equally blamed for their
attempts to do both.

Anyway, in October 1929 the stock market cracked and the
decline set in in earnest. By 1932, for the world as a whole,
wholesale prices (measured in gold) and industrial production
had each fallen by about a third, employment and the volume
of international trade by about a quarter below their 1929 levels.
Behind these bare figures lies a long story of disorder and
distress. Nationally and internationally, the rush for cover,
the struggle to be 'liquid' at all and anybody's cost, raged for a
time almost unchecked. Firms reduced their commitments;
banks called in their loans at home and abroad; Governments
strove to reduce their expenditures; speculators flung their
money about the world looking no longer for profits but for
that unpluckable flower, safety. The world's hard-won monetary unity broke down under the strain. In 1930, Australia
and New Zealand showed the way, which so many were to
follow, through the gap of exchange depreciation. In the
spring of 1931 the Central European economy blew up; the
German banks, deeply involved in the fortunes of their
country's industries, collapsed; and the reparation and war
debt settlements crumbled. In September 1931 the Bank of
England, under the pressure of the withdrawal of foreign funds
from London, suspended the delivery of gold bullion in exchange for its notes (p. 54); and the pound sterling, followed
immediately or after a short interval by many of the rest of the
world's monetary units, was cast loose once more on the ocean
of fluctuating exchanges.

In the United States the depression continued to deepen;
by 1932 industrial production had sunk to little above half its
1929 level, and the number of unemployed is said to have
reached 14 million. There, moreover, in contrast to England,

the thirst for safety could not be assuaged by anything so im-
palpable as bank money, but reached out after common
money and even hard metal.   The weaker among the twenty-
four thousand separate banks began to explode at a great rate,
and by the time (March 1933) that the new President,
Roosevelt, took office matters had reached such a pass that it
was thought wiser to close the doors of every bank in the
country.   There followed a curious episode.   As part of the
complicated and not wholly self-consistent pattern of recovery
measures which came to be known as the New Deal, the dollar
itself was detached from gold, and for a time gold was bought
by the authorities at gradually rising dollar prices.   Not until
January 1934 was the dollar tied up again to gold, and then at
a parity some 40 per cent below the old one.

§ 2. The Scramble to Recovery.   A Martian who had left this
planet in disgust in 1932 and returned to visit it in the spring of
1937 would probably have been astonished at the degree of
recovery which had been achieved during his absence.   He
would have found the United States once more in a state of
boom, though he would still have been able to count some
millions of unemployed persons within her frontiers.   He
would have found Britain still in difficulty over some of her
out-dated industries, but covered with a rash of nice new houses
and not a few new factories, and back at her old game of doing
other people's business and looking after other people's money;
for while the old gold exchange system had perished in the
flames, a relatively compact and like-minded group of nations
had been found very ready to adhere to the *sterling* exchange
system which had arisen from its ashes.   Peeping over the
high walls, our Martian might perhaps have got a glimpse of
the wheels of reconstruction and rearmament whirring in
Germany and the Soviet Union.   Everywhere he looked he
would have seen, indeed, an incredible proliferation of trade
restrictions and controls of many different kinds; yet the volume
of world trade, he would have learnt, was almost back at its
1929 level.   Nor did its further recovery seem likely to be

threatened by a fresh wave of exchange instability. Wobbling exchanges, after being all the rage, had once more become unfashionable. The two main blocks, dollar and sterling, after their bout of mutual sparring for position, had settled down to a somewhat frigid *modus vivendi*, whose stabilising influence had now become effective also over a wider area. But poor France, racked by an instability of political and social forces graver even than that of the exchanges, was still about to take a fresh bite at that cherry of devaluation which, in company with Switzerland and Holland, she had left hanging too long upon the tree. And in countries farther east—and above all in Germany—more radical changes had been taking place. There a free market in foreign money, of the kind whose existence was taken for granted when this book was written in 1928, had been abolished altogether. All demands for and supplies of foreign moneys were centralised in official hands. The value of each several sort of foreign money was fixed separately in terms of the home money in accordance with all kinds of commercial and other considerations; and even the same foreign money might have a different value, in terms of the home money, for different purposes. Thus over all this part of the world—and the same was true to some extent of South America—there had grown up a network of special arrangements between pairs of States, described as 'payments agreements' or 'clearing agreements' according to their exact technical details, whose effect was to concentrate the flow of trade in particular channels. These arrangements were much criticised by those whose desire to participate in the trade of these countries was thus thwarted; but they were defended by those who practised them on the ground that some trade is better than no trade at all—which to countries shorn of their international monetary reserves by the storm of 1929–32 had seemed for a time to be the most likely alternative.

Our supposed visitor would have been able to listen to many opinions as to how the world had been enabled to make such a relatively good showing. Was it just that in 1932 the trade cycle, in obedience to the mysterious laws of its own being, had rounded the corner, and that neither blundering governments nor defective institutions could altogether stay its upward course? Was it, on the contrary, due precisely to that fact that in the leading countries positive 'interventionist' policies of one kind or another—the adventurous farrago of the New Deal, the marriage of misty Nazi ideology with the highly practical ingenuities of Dr. Schacht, English neo-Toryism with its new-fangled apparatus of marketing boards and its all-powerful Import Duties Advisory Committee—had replaced the previous régimes of inertia and drift? Or was the predominant part of the truth of an intermediate and more strictly monetary kind, deserving therefore of special attention from the writer and readers of this little book? Certain it is that, acting in echelon and standing on one another's shoulders to do it, most of the countries of the world had by now done what it has often been suggested in retrospect that they would have been wiser to do in concert. They had relaxed, though with greatly varying alacrity and thoroughness, their notions and practices with regard to the links to be maintained between their money supplies and gold; and they had increased, though in proportions varying from 25 per cent (Holland) to 200 per cent (Japan), the value of gold in terms of their local moneys. Thus they had given themselves more elbow-room and power of manœuvre—increased freedom at least to experiment how much or how little the dishing out of money on easy terms would do (p. 147) to re-create a flow of monetary demand. Nor was it only their existing reserves which had thus acquired the magic property of reproduction by fission. The rise in the money prices offered for gold by the Western countries had led by 1937 to a rise of some 80 per cent in its annual rate of output above the level of 1929; and in addition the peoples of India and China, taking the profit on what had been derided as a stupid habit but had turned out to be a pretty good invest-ment, had regurgitated out of their hoards the equivalent of more than twice the 1929 output. Not all this new or re-born gold had gone where it would have been of most use; but the fears of progress being held back by an *absolute* shortage of gold, which had oppressed some observers in 1928–30 (p. 118), seemed to have been effectually removed.

§ **3. The Morrow of War.**   Another little recession and another recovery in production and trade, but an uncomfortable one, dominated by armament production and by trade in the war metals.   The mobile money of Europe streaming once more across the Atlantic in quest of safety.   And then, in September 1939, war and destruction once more, and on a grander scale even than before.   Let us give our Martian leave of absence (fortunate fellow) for the grim war years, and summon him back for another look round in the early months of 1947.   He will find some pre-war trends reversed and others accentuated. Gold production, for instance, diminished again—there are more useful weapons than gold in war, at any rate in a Lend-Lease war, and it is the one thing whose price in the leading moneys has remained almost or quite unchanged, while its money costs of production have risen sharply.   The East once more gulping down, though not so avidly as during the war itself, whatever scraps of gold it can get hold of.   The quantity of money—bank money, common money—everywhere greatly increased as a result of conjuring tricks in war finance similar in nature to, though sometimes different in technical detail from, those whose operation in the First Great Muddle has already been described (Ch. VI).   Prices everywhere higher than in 1939, but here by more and there by less, and hardly anywhere in proportion to the increase in the stock of money. In some unfortunate countries, indeed, our visitor would learn, a thunder-and-lightning sequence like that described on p. 98 had carried the monetary unit out through the ceiling, like the 'thing' whose movements Alice tried to follow in the Sheep's shop: thus the pengö (p. 106), having multiplied itself 300,000 million million million million times, disappeared in 1946 in a cloud of smoke.   Some countries, on the other hand, such as Belgium, to be on the safe side, had firmly hacked a bit off their inflated money supply by freezing part of everybody's holdings, both of bank and common money, into State loans.   But most,

in order to keep the spending proclivities of firms and individuals within bounds, seemed to be ready to go on trusting to
one or both of two powerful aids—direct systems of rationing
and control and a continued non-availability of many of the
things which firms and individuals would really have liked to
buy.   Everywhere there was a firm resolve to prevent, by
stringent controls of the international movement of private
capital, a repetition of the havoc wrought by the wandering
greed-money and funk-money of 1921–3, 1931, and 1938–9.
And partly with this end in view and partly because world
scarcities of many necessary things were still compelling the
maintenance of the siege economies of war-time, most countries
outside the United States were still maintaining that centralised
and selective administration of the market for foreign moneys
which had been confined in the 1930's to a group of European
and South American countries (p. 157), but had become common form on the outbreak of war.

§ 4. Changes in the Rules.   In most countries the link between
money and gold had become more elastic even than in the
thirties, and much of the classification of the kinds of money
and monetary system given in Chapters III and IV of this book
now wears rather a faded air, though it has not, the writer
hopes, lost its interest as history or its usefulness as an aid to
clearness of thought.   It must be enough, in a book of this
scale, to indicate briefly what has happened to the rules of the
monetary game in England and the United States since we last
watched them functioning in 1928.   To begin with the relation
between bank deposits and bank reserves (p. 42).   In England
this is still a matter of convention, not of law, but towards the
end of 1946 the convention was at last enshrined in a public
statement, and it was made plain that the proportion there
named, namely 8 per cent, was to be effectively maintained day
by day—a thing which previously, in the case of most of the
banks, had been far from true of the periodically published
figure of 10 or 11 per cent.   More than two-thirds of these
reserves now consists of a balance with the Bank of England,

and to these 'bankers' balances' the Bank's reserve in its own notes bears a proportion which rushes about in a wild and meaningless fashion and is much lower than of old.   In the United States the legal prescription of *minimum* percentage reserves (p. 46) did not prevent the banks belonging to the system (whose resources are now five-sixths of those of all commercial banks) from piling up large reserves in excess of the legal minimum in the unconfident years of the early 1930's. In order to increase their powers of control in the short, sharp boom of 1936–7, the authorities used (by stages) their lately acquired power to double the legal minima, thus mopping up the greater part of the 'excess reserves.'   Thereafter the legal minima were changed several times in accordance with varying situations, and since 1942 have stood at 6 per cent for time deposits and at a figure which now works out, on the average for the various classes of banks, at about 18 per cent of demand deposits.   This power of varying the legal minima was re-garded at one time as a very useful weapon of central bank control.

Now let us see what has happened to common money in the two countries since 1928.   The Bank of England note has not been legally convertible into anything whatever since September 1931, and it is not easy to say what the singular statement in-scribed on its face—'I promise to pay the bearer on demand the sum of one pound'—really means (one ribald writer has sug-gested that what the chief cashier is promising to do is to give you a new note in exchange for any note whose number seems to you to be an unlucky one).   As regards reserve rules, the old forms established by the Acts of 1844 and 1928 (p. 51) have been conserved, but the reality has been changed beyond recognition by the concentration of the country's gold holdings in the hands not of the Bank but of the Government, and by the use in ways never originally intended of the powers reserved in the Act of 1928 to vary the amount of the Bank's 'fiduciary issue.'   Here, in briefest outline, is the story.   When the pound was cast loose from gold in 1931, the market price of gold swung smartly up above the level of 85s. per fine ounce

(77s. 9d. per standard ounce, p. 54) which the Bank was obliged to pay and at which its store of gold was still valued. Not many months later the tide began to turn—people abroad began to feel that English money had become too cheap and to want to buy it again. At this point there was set up a special Government fund called the Exchange Equalisation Account, with power to buy gold at the market price. This served several purposes, of which two are here to the point. First, by incurring a book loss it could hand on to the Bank some of its gold purchases, thus enabling the Bank, without departure from received ideas about the significance of the fiduciary issue (which was actually *reduced* to £200 million), to expand its *total* note issue in consonance with the policy of 'easy money' and trade expansion which was being pursued. Secondly, by not handing on *all* the gold which it bought, it could build up a useful nest-egg against the possibility that the people who were now wanting to buy English money should some day want to sell it again. If that day should come, it would be highly convenient to satisfy their demands without withdrawing gold from the base of the domestic monetary pyramid, which is what would have had to be done under a full gold standard.

As the war-clouds gathered over Europe, come that day did, and early in 1939 further changes were made. About two-thirds of the Bank's gold was swept into the depleted coffers (exactly *how* depleted, we have never yet been told) of the Exchange Equalisation Account; the gap was filled partly by fixing the fiduciary issue at £300 million (after a preliminary wobble up to £400 million) and partly by revaluing the remainder of the Bank's gold at the market price of 148s. 5d., the Bank's obligation to buy gold at 85s. being abolished. Further, the new Act recognised not only that the price of gold *had* altered but that it might alter again in future, and laid down that the Bank's gold should continuously be revalued to match. The limits of human ingenuity in pouring new wine into old bottles—in making the movements of the nominal regulator conform to those of the thing to be regulated—seemed to have been reached. And had peace prevailed, there the story might have rested; but as it was there was more to follow. On the outbreak of war in September 1939 the whole of the Bank's remaining gold, save for a paltry £100,000, was shifted into the Exchange Account, so as to be all dressed up and ready to cross the Atlantic in payment for munitions of war. Thus virtually the whole outstanding note issue of just over £580 million attained the dignity of fiduciariness. That august status it still retains, while as a result of successive uses of the powers conferred by the 1928 Act the £580 million, by the end of 1946, had grown to £1450 million. The Account still stands ready to buy gold, at a price which throughout the war was fixed at 168s. and has now been raised to 172s. 3d. Its holding of gold alone has not been published for any date later than September 1938; but its holding of gold and United States dollars, after sinking to a very low level during the first 18 months of war, stood at £642 million in December 1946.

In the United States, the complicated pattern of common moneys alluded to (though not set out in full) on p. 51 has been subjected to a process of simplification. That process is not yet complete; but about 80 per cent of the common money in the hands of the public and the ordinary banks now consists of Federal Reserve notes, and another 7 per cent of silver certificates. In the early days of the New Deal, steps were taken to call in from circulation all gold coins and gold certificates, and to transfer all gold from the Federal Reserve Banks to the Treasury and substitute a new type of gold certificate, issued in exchange for this gold, as the entity of which the Reserve Banks must hold minimum percentage amounts against both their notes and deposits (p. 46). These percentages were not relaxed during the depression, as they were in most countries which had adopted the percentage system (in totalitarian Germany and Italy they were abolished altogether); in the United States it was not till 1945 that, to oil the wheels of war finance in its closing stages, they were both reduced to 25. Since 1933 the Federal Reserve notes have been legal tender, and it seems that they must now be classed as definitive money not convertible (p. 41); for in view of the fact that they are now themselves 'lawful money' it does not seem possible to attach much sense to the provision, which has survived from earlier days, that they are 'redeemable in lawful money' at the Treasury or at any Reserve Bank. Nor, since the Gold Reserve Act of January 1934 abolished gold coinage, is it easy to attach any very clear meaning to the provision of that Act fixing 'the weight of the gold dollar' at some point, to be decided by the President, between 50 and 60 per cent of the old gold parity, or to the President's decision that that percentage should be 59·06. The operative instrument retaining the United States from 1934 onwards on what has commonly been described as a gold standard seems to have been the announcement by the Secretary of the Treasury that he would in fact be willing to buy gold at about the corresponding price of 35 dollars per fine ounce, and to release it at about the same price to certain selected Central Banks—though reserving the right to change the price, or suspend the arrangement altogether, virtually without notice.

§ **5. The New Monetary Club.** Throughout the tangled course of monetary history in these sensational years there can be discerned running two different-coloured threads—two conflicting influences pulling this way and that in the counsels of the nations and even in the thoughts and utterances and acts of those outstanding individuals—a Roosevelt, a Keynes—to whom fell a specially large share in the guidance of events. On the one hand a resolve to make money a servant and not a master of national economic policy—whether that policy was devoted primarily to the healing of distress, to preparation for war, to the efficient conduct of a war-time siege economy, or to post-war recuperation. On the other hand a recognition that no nation can live to itself alone, and that if all nations are determined to hoist themselves up on each other's shoulders, it is all too likely that all of them will go down in the mud. These two threads are plainly visible in that complicated instrument officially known as the Final Act of the United

Nations Monetary and Financial Conference, 1944, which the nations then on the high road to victory forged for the better ordering of the world's post-war monetary affairs, and out of which were born in 1946 two new institutions—an International Monetary Fund and an International Bank for Reconstruction and Development.   The forty-four nations which have so far adhered to the former have each of them declared (or in a few cases undertaken soon to declare) a 'par value' for their monetary units in terms of gold or of 'the United States dollar of the weight and fineness in effect on July 1, 1944' (that *rara avis* which, since it is forbidden to be hatched (p. 166), nobody has ever yet seen).   These par values they have reserved the collective right (though only if the United States and Britain individually agree) to change in concert in either direction, thus forestalling the criticism that they have bound their fortunes irrevocably to the vagaries of the wayward yellow metal (p. 119). Such a change is not at present to be anticipated; apart from it, and apart from certain initial adjustments in special cases, the nations must not seek to change their par values except 'to correct a fundamental disequilibrium'; nor even then, if the desired change exceeds 10 per cent, make it off their own bat without consent of the authorities of the Fund—unless indeed they are prepared to be required to leave the Club.   Exchange stability they must promote, competitive exchange alterations and those bugbears of the Schachtian epoch, 'discriminating currency arrangements and multiple currency practices', they must eschew.   'Restrictions on the making of payments and transfers for current international transactions' they may not impose.   And to help him to keep the rules, each member may dip his fingers, within limitations and under conditions too complex for summary here, into a pool worth (on the basis of the present membership of the Club) some £1,920 million—a pool consisting partly (say, £330 million) of gold and partly of claims to the money of each of his fellow-members.   By so dipping, it is hoped, he may be able to rub along, through periods in which his power of earning what he is in the habit of buying from the outside world is for some reason temporarily depressed, without trying to keep his account straight by 'resorting to measures destructive of national or international prosperity.'

Here is fine work to be done: but will it not break the back of the young heifer to whom it has been allotted if she is expected also to give milk—the milk needed to bring the war-stricken nations back into that normal state of health in which they can seriously tackle the task of balancing, with no more than moderate and temporary lapses, their accounts in respect of those 'current international transactions'? It was this anxiety, anxiety lest the Fund should be turned into too much of what the farmers call a dual-purpose animal, which led to the installation, in an adjoining crib of the Washington stable, of a companion animal, the International Bank. She it is who is to provide the main draughts of milk for the reconstruction of old countries and the development of so-called new ones. This milk she is to yield partly out of the flesh that has been put on her by the nations who joined together to give her life (the self-same Club as owns the Fund), but mainly as a result of grazing around (with a bell round her neck to show her high birth and breeding) in the private investment markets of the richer members of the Club. As this chapter is being written there are orders for some £575 million worth of milk outside her stall, while only a faint lowing has yet been heard from within: but these are early days.[1] Meanwhile special provision has been made in other ways for some immediate needs. In particular, an attempt has been made to look after the immediate needs of Britain, joint linchpin of the two Clubs, by dollar loans equivalent to some £930 million from the United States and some £310 million from Canada: though this provision now looks less adequate than it did when it was arranged, since American prices have risen sharply, and since the temporary annexation by Britain, in a fit of absence of mind, of a large slice of Germany is involving her in a heavy expenditure of dollars.

[1] A jug of milk worth £62 million has now (May, 1947) been supplied to France.

To return to heifer Fund; there are other provisions too for keeping within bounds the demands to be made on her, especially in her salad days.   She not only need not, she *must* not, carry capital uphill; the nations have promised not to try to load that greed-money and funk-money (p. 162) upon her back.   The 'transfers and payments for current transactions' which must not be restricted, and the making of which are therefore a potential cause of recourse to the Fund, do not include—go slowly here, reader—the expenditure by A, for current imports from B, of C-money owned by A as the result of war-time expenditure by C on the products or services of A. They do not include, for instance, the expenditure on American goods of the £1200 million of claims to English money now held by the Reserve Bank of India; such matters are left to be dealt with by special arrangement between the parties concerned.   More generally, a breathing space is to be allowed before that forswearing of restrictions on current payments comes into force, though the patient's lung-power is to remain under careful observation by Dr. Fund, and though Britain, as part of the conditions of her loan from the United States, has undertaken to learn to breathe normally by July 1947. Again, in the event of one country's money being in such keen demand by its neighbours that the Fund's supplies of it look like running out, provision is made for a share-out of what remains and for resumption by each country of liberty to reduce its demands for that money by whatever means it thinks fit. Finally, it is to be noted that the whole instrument deals only with restrictions of a specifically monetary kind—restrictions on 'payments and transfers'; nothing is said about direct limitations on the import of goods.   It has, however, been agreed that the spirit of the instrument demands that an attempt shall be made to tackle this matter also on parallel lines; and at the time this chapter is being written the first overt steps in this direction have lately been taken.

What is at the back of the elaborate precautions with which the nations have thus hedged about their adhesion to the new Monetary Club, and which will doubtless figure equally largely in the new Trade Club if and when it is born? A main part of the answer is to be found in the outstanding wealth and economic power of one of the members. The reader will remember that even in 1928 it was tempting to say that the United States was on a privately managed standard of her own and the rest of the world on a dollar standard (p. 67); and though the event showed that the managers of the American standard, whether or not they were all-wise, were far from all-powerful, the forces attracting the world's monetary reserves in her direction continued to grow in strength. As a result first of the withdrawal of her own lendings from Europe and of the flight of European funk-money which followed in their wake, and later of the pressing desire of the war-involved nations to buy her goods, her gold stock trebled in weight between 1928 and 1941 and came to constitute some two-thirds of the monetary gold stock of the whole world (outside the Soviet Union). By the end of 1946, as a result mainly of the help given to her Allies through the Lend-Lease system and of sundry post-war gifts and loans, it had fallen by a tenth and its proportion to the world stock to perhaps not much over half; while apart from such further loans as she may make, directly or through the International Club, some nations hold in their own right substantial dollar balances and other easily realisable assets within her borders, upon which they will be able to draw to balance their accounts. Nevertheless, looking a little farther ahead, anxiety remains widespread as to how far she can so change and control her habits as to become a lavish and consistent buyer of what the world has to offer, in goods and services, in exchange for her products. For unless she can, however generously she fills the gap in the near future by loans, in the long run the service of those loans will only add another element of unbalance to cause a creaking in the joints of the new quasi-gold standard. It is the writer's duty to record the inauguration of the Club movement (*cujus pars minima fuit*) and his pleasure to wish it every success; but it is beyond his powers to predict, in this spring of 1947, whether it carries within it the seeds of a real and lasting monetary unity of the world.

CHAPTER X

PROBLEMS OF WORDS, THOUGHT AND ACTION

'It's really dreadful,' she muttered to herself, 'the way all
the creatures argue.   It's enough to drive one crazy.'
Alice's Adventures in Wonderland

§ 1. Prices and Output.   The sensational events of the last
eighteen years have naturally given a great stimulus to thought
and argument about monetary affairs; and if you are passing
on from this little book to make a thorough study of recent
monetary theory you will find yourself in a jungle of controversy, some of it highly sophisticated and not a little of it,
I fear, rather acrimonious.   I cannot go with you through the
jungle, nor attempt to summarise here what I have written about
these matters in another book, which, of course, I should like
you to read.[1]   But I should not like to let you enter the jungle
altogether unprepared; and in this last chapter I must try to
give you an idea of what some of these controversies are about
—speaking, as you will already have noticed, in the first person
singular in order to hammer it in that these are difficult matters
about which people are still disputing, and that you must make
up your mind about them for yourself after hearing what other
people have to say.   But perhaps, if you are able to make
allowance for the cantankerousness of academic persons and
the little vested interests they acquire in words and phrases,
you will come to the conclusion that they often do not really
differ as much as they like to think.

In the first place, then, you will find some talk going on as

[1] *Essays in Monetary Theory*, 1940, reprinted 1946 (Staples Press),
especially number XI, 'A Survey of Modern Monetary Controversy.'

to what monetary theory is all about and how it should be approached. Now in the second chapter of this book I followed tradition in treating the *value* of money as the centre of my picture, exhibiting it as the resultant of various forces of demand and supply, among the forces of demand being the level of the real national income or output (p. 24). This practice has been condemned by some modern writers, one of whom[1] once went so far as to say that 'the economists' had been 'misled into supposing that the proper subject of the so-called theory of money was the level of prices and not the volume of output,' and to suggest, if I understand aright, that we ought to have two separate compartments of thought, one a theory of money proper and the other a theory of output or employment. Reader, I do not think that I was 'misled' or that I misled you! I told you very early (p. 12) that one of the chief reasons for our concern at the instability of the value of money was its connection with trade depression and unemployment, and I warned you (p. 32 and App. A, II) that, when we are studying processes of change, the demand for money and its supply cannot be taken as independent forces, since they act and re-act upon one another. It was perhaps natural for those writing in the early thirties, on the morrow of the great slump, to lay special stress on the extreme case in which an expansion of monetary demand will exercise the whole of its effect in raising output and employment and none of it in raising prices.[2] But we cannot draw a hard-and-fast line, as some have sought to do, between what happens when there are unemployed resources and what happens when there is something more or less arbitrarily defined as 'full employment'; in

[1] Joan Robinson, in *Review of Economic Studies*, 1933–4, p. 26.

[2] A rather similar situation seems to have prevailed in the United Kingdom in 1894–6, when the first effects of large imports of gold seem to have been purely sedative and medicinal; on the other hand, after the recession of 1908 the first phase of revival mainly took the form of a highly speculative rise in the prices of raw materials: see my *Study of Industrial Fluctuation*, pp. 229–31. There is nothing new under the sun; but the lessons of history are not always easy to read or to apply to contemporary situations.

the fashionable jargon of 1947, 'bottlenecks' may begin to appear at any stage in an industrial revival. It does not, of course, follow that the kinds of expansory policy briefly commended on p. 145ff. should be called off as soon as the first bottleneck rises above the horizon, any more than it follows that they should be carried on until the last bottleneck has been ironed out. But in guiding our judgment as to just how far they should be pressed, there is no room for two separate branches of economic theory, a 'theory of money' and a 'theory of output.' If we like to put it so, what may appear at the very bottom of the slump to be a theory of output alone soon passes insensibly into a theory of prices *and* output and ends up as a theory of prices alone. Reader, I do not think that on reflection you will blame me for starting you off on your troubled voyage with a little piece of apparatus which I warned you (p. 23) was more easily applied in comparing relatively stable and serene situations than in analysing processes of disturbance, though with a little ingenuity, as I tried to show, it can be adapted to the latter as well.

§ **2. Saving and Capital Outlay.** Now I come to a matter on which, to speak frankly, I think a number of people have created a lot of unnecessary confusion. But I will lead up to this charge by sitting for a moment in a white, or fairly white, sheet myself. In describing the way in which the banking system can procure the building up of an increment of material capital by inflicting a burden on the public in the shape of rising prices, I followed a number of earlier writers in labelling this burden with the name 'forced saving' (pp. 74–76, cf. p. 130). Perhaps I should have been wiser to follow another writer, Professor Pigou, in giving it the more noncommittal name of a 'forced levy.' Perhaps too I should have done well to make it plainer than I have done on pp. 74–76 that in our existing society, where some money incomes respond easily to changes in prices while others are very sticky (p. 9), the burden is likely to be borne predominantly by one set of people while the 'saved' increment of money balances belongs predominantly to another. What I cannot agree to is the view that this whole notion of 'some species of levy on the public, called "forced saving" or the like,' possesses no validity whatever, and is indeed to be classed among 'the worst muddles of all'![1]   And it follows from what I have said in § 1 above that I do not regard the validity of this notion of a levy as confined to the case which I illustrated on pp. 74–76 —the case in which monetary expansion stimulates no increase at all in the current output of consumption goods, so that their prices rise in full proportion to the increase in the stream of monetary demand.   In less extreme cases there will also be levies, though of smaller amounts.   But neither in the extreme case nor in the more general case are we bound, or indeed entitled, to leap to the conclusion that in all circumstances such a levy is necessarily on the balance 'a bad thing' (p. 116).

The reasoning which seems to lie behind the view to which I have just taken exception has been put in simple language as follows:[2]   'All incomes are derived either from producing consumption goods or from producing investment goods.   And all income either is spent on consumption goods or is saved. The income derived from producing consumption goods is equal to what is spent on them.   Therefore what is saved is equal to the income derived from producing investment goods. In short, the rate of saving is equal to the rate of investment.' Evidently, if we define our terms suitably (and this involves, among other things, counting increments of circulating capital (p. 85) as investment goods—a point to which I shall return), this statement is true, because it is what is called a tautology. Now we must not despise tautologies, which are sometimes very serviceable animals.   But I am sure that to lay emphasis on this particular specimen of the tribe is very apt to confuse our judgment.   Here for instance is the way in which the tautology (whose discovery he attributes to 'modern economic research') is stated by a recent distinguished convert[3] to the

[1] Keynes, *General Theory of Employment, Interest and Money*, p. 183.

[2] Joan Robinson, *Introduction to the Theory of Employment*, p. 8.

[3] Beveridge, *Full Employment in a Free Society*, p. 337.

order of ideas which it is used to support: 'capital expenditure itself brings into existence the very savings necessary to finance it.' Now does not that sentence cry out for completion in some such words as these—'and therefore can never be carried on on an excessive scale'? Yet we know that the latter is not true. The expenditure of the German army in Greece (for Government deficits and the like count as honorary 'investment' in this connection) brought into existence the very savings necessary to finance it in the sense that at every moment *some* poor devil was holding each of the thousand-drachma notes poured out in such generous profusion on to the markets! If we restate this great tautology in some less tendentious form such as this, 'all money which is anywhere must indeed be somewhere,' we shall perhaps see more clearly that, however much 'modern economic research' may have gone to its making, it is utterly barren unless we probe behind it to see what is really happening in any particular case, as I tried to do, in a chatty and imprecise way, in the sundry little tales which I told in my Chapter V.

This truth seems indeed to be floating about in the subconscious of the writers whom I am discussing, for they often pass, without realising apparently what they are doing, from affirming the great tautology (which, of course, *must* be fulfilled in any slice of time, however short and however disturbed) into doing something quite different. They assert, namely—keep your head, reader—that a given once-for-all increase in the rate of capital outlay per unit of time will, after an interval, be found to have generated just so large an increase in the rate of money income received per unit of time that the rate of additional money saving per unit of time will thereafter be equal to the additional rate of capital outlay per unit of time with which the story started, no *further* expansion of money income taking place and the economy proceeding thereafter on an even keel. Thus Mrs. Robinson, having explained in the passage which I have quoted how the amount of saving and the amount of capital outlay, being defined so as to be identical, must always at every level of income indeed be equal, goes on a

13

few pages later to explain (the italics are mine) how 'the increase in incomes must necessarily continue *up to the point at which* there is an addition to saving equal to the additional [capital] outlay.'[1]   Reader, do you see what has happened? An assertion that two quantities are by definition identical has been transmuted into an assertion that the establishment of equality between them is a *condition of equilibrium*.   It seems to me that this is very confusing, and that I have not been unfair in comparing economists who write in this way to a naturalist who, having defined an elephant's trunk and its proboscis in identical terms, should then go on to explain the profound biological forces which tend to adjust the size of the trunk to the size of the proboscis.

Your first step, then, when you meet these authors in the jungle, will have to be to do a piece of tidying-up which they might well have done for you.   You will have to explain to yourself that when the equality of 'saving' and 'investment' is being treated no longer as an identity but as a condition of equilibrium, the meaning of the word 'saving' has been subtly transformed, so that it no longer means the part of to-day's income which people actually fail to spend on consumption, but the part of to-day's income which they *intend* not to spend, or perhaps (which may come to much the same thing) the part of *yesterday's* income which they fail to spend.   And thereby hangs a similar tale about the companion word 'investment.' I pointed out that in the version of the great tautology which I quoted, it is necessary to define 'capital goods' so as to include increments of goods, of whatever kind, in process of production or in store.   Now we need not boggle at that so long as we are merely dealing with the tautology.   Nor need we boggle at it at all so long as the increments of goods in process or in store are *designed*, like that building up of an apple-crop which formed the subject of my illustration in Chapter V.   But when we come to discuss conditions of equilibrium, there is obviously a great difference between this sort of designed increase of circulating capital and a piling-up of goods in factories and shops

[1] Op. cit., p. 21.

because, owing to a falling-off in money demand, the owners are not able to dispose of them as easily as they expected. Such a state of affairs, and the opposite state of affairs in which stores of goods are being depleted *faster* than was intended or expected, are obviously evidences of a *lack* of equilibrium, even though for the moment neither prices nor output is changing; for they are a sure sign that a change in one or the other is in the offing. So it is equality of *designed* or *intended* 'investment,' not of *actual* 'investment,' with designed saving that can be regarded as a condition of equilibrium.

But having tidied up all this as best you can, and with the aid of whatever company of words you prefer (only you must not change their meaning in the middle of an argument), you must do your best to examine candidly and carefully the important question of substance that lies behind. How far is it likely to be possible for a community, by means of an increase in capital outlay, to advance from a stable or equilibrium position in which output and employment are low to a new stable or equilibrium position in which they are higher and indeed to one in which employment can reasonably be described as 'full'? There is so much to be said about this problem that if I were to begin to discuss it thoroughly with you I should soon be filling another book. I will not even write down here —for you will find it in many other books—the little piece of algebra which serves in some expositions as a magic carpet to waft us from one platform to the next. When you make its acquaintance, you will have to ask yourself a number of questions. There is a key-piece in the formula—a fraction representing the proportion of additional money income received in the preceding slice of time which people will desire or intend to save in *this* slice of time. Would it be reasonable to take this fraction as remaining constant throughout the process of expansion even if prices were to remain unchanged, so that a given increment of total money income meant an equivalent increment of total *real* income? And what exactly are we to suppose to happen when prices begin to rise, so that a given increment of total money income means a smaller and

smaller increment of total real income? Again, is it right to
regard all the money saved at each stage as becoming available
to 'finance' the assumed original addition to the rate of capital
outlay, or will some of it, especially if it is saved by joint-stock
companies and people running their own businesses, walk off
on its own to 'finance' quite different pieces of capital outlay?
You must think over such problems as best you can, and we
must all try to keep an open mind until those latter-day
wizards, the econometricians, have had more opportunity to
see if they can throw a steady light on them. But my own
feeling, for what it is worth, is that in this so-called 'marginal
propensity to save' (not very happily called, as I think, for the
'propensity to save' depends on other things besides recently
acquired income—on capital wealth, for instance, and especially
perhaps on the proportion of capital wealth which is ready to
hand and easy to spend) we have a potentially useful little
brick, but not yet a very firm foundation for that imposing
edifice of combined prosperity and stability which we should
all like to build if only we knew how.

§ 3. **Hoarding and Dishoarding.** There is another little verbal
trap waiting for you in the jungle about which I should like to
offer a word. Though I did not use it in my book, I think it
is often convenient to describe by the term 'hoarding' that
process of turning money aside from active use which contracts
the stream of money demand and so tends to cause depression
and unemployment. For some reason which I have never been
able to understand this word makes some writers very angry,
and they would like to banish it from the economic vocabulary.
I do not think you should be put off by this, for it is a simple
and expressive little word; but you must be careful to use it in
a sense which does not invite criticism. The definition which
I gave a good many years ago,[1] and which I think a number of
people have found acceptable, is this: a person (and 'person'
includes composite persons, such as joint-stock companies)

[1] 'Saving and Hoarding,' in *Economic Journal*, 1933, p. 400; reprinted
in *Essays in Monetary Theory*.

may be said to hoard in any period if he takes steps to increase the proportion existing at the beginning of that period between his money stock and his money income. A simple case of hoarding occurs if a man saves part of his income and leaves it on current account at a bank; but you will observe that this is by no means the only kind of case covered by my definition. Thus a person—whether he be a professional dealer or an ordinary investor—who sells some securities without passing on the proceeds in purchasing other securities is hoarding. So is a business which raises money from the public and puts it aside till it is ready to expend it on labour or materials or machines. Anybody is hoarding who does something 'calculated,' as the police would say, to cause a hitch up in the flow of money income—a decrease in the income velocity of circulation of money (p. 27). Hoarding by ordinary persons and businesses and money-destruction by banks and Governments cover between them, if we like to put it so, the actions by which the designed capital outlay per unit of time is caused to fall short of designed saving per unit of time. You can easily frame for yourself a corresponding set of statements about dishoarding, and I think you will agree that anyone who takes the trouble to get hold of this idea need not get hot and bothered about what one writer has been pleased to call 'the fallacy of hoarding.'

§ **4. Depression and Stagnation.** I want now to point out frankly two big differences in climate or temperature which you will probably sense between the book which you have just read and many of the more recent books to which you will now pass on. The first is concerned with the strength of the forces making for industrial depression, the second with the rôle of Government in overcoming them.

I do not think that if you glance again at pp. 12–13 you will feel that it needed the great depression of the 1930's to persuade me or my generation of the evils of mass unemployment. But it is true that when I came to write my Chapter V about the mechanics of banking and my Chapter VIII about 'the question

of the cycle' I gave most of my space to pointing out the
dangers of what is commonly called inflation and discussing
the possible methods of keeping it in control. Perhaps that
will not seem so odd or wrong-headed to you, my first new
readers in 1947, as it doubtless did to your predecessors in the
1930's; for you have had a taste of the peculiar troubles of a
period of 'full employment,' now sometimes rather ungrate-
fully re-christened as 'shortage of man-power.' But troubles
of this kind were not really very acute when I was writing in
1928; and if I laid so much stress on control of the boom it
was rather because I had shaken down to what I was then
justified in calling the 'common opinion' that, if this could
be successfully achieved, there was good hope that the worst
evils of trade depression could thereby be averted (p. 145).
In short, to speak rather loosely, for it is no use trying to use
very precise language over this, I shared the view that depression was a recurrent rather than an endemic malady, though
one very closely tied into the secular processes of growth and
capital investment.

Now it is that standpoint which we have all of us got to
review in the light of the queerness of some of the happenings
of the 1920's (p. 156), of the extreme violence of the slump of
the early 1930's, and of the incompleteness of the recovery
therefrom in the latter years of the decade. Reflecting on
these things, many able minds have been converted to what has
come to be called the 'stagnation thesis'—the doctrine that
the societies of the West have reached a stage of affluence and
technical development in which the desire to save is *chronically*
outrunning the openings and inducements for fresh enterprise
and innovation, so that, unless very strong steps are taken to
contrive otherwise, depression will henceforth be the normal
order of the day, punctuated only by little wisps and flickers of
partial and abortive recovery. It is fair to point out that such
prophecies have been made before and have not in fact been
fulfilled, Dame Nature or Dame History having always in the
end turned out to be keeping another card up her sleeve,
though she has sometimes been rather long in shaking it down.

But that does not absolve us from trying to assess afresh the probabilities that this time the wolf of stagnation really is on the doorstep, or at any rate prowling in the near neighbourhood and ready to start gnawing at our vitals as soon as the processes of post-war reconstruction, which for the time being have naturally transformed the picture, are complete.

There is more to be said about this problem than it would be any use trying to pack into a few sentences in this short supplementary chapter;[1] nor should you worry if, when you have studied it more fully, you still feel unable to give a clear-cut answer to a question which, after all, can only even be asked in a rather vague and symbolic form. But it will be all to the good if you read many writings in which the technique of *positive* action to promote 'a high and stable level' of activity and employment, as the official phrase now runs, receives much more ample discussion than it did in my little book. Meanwhile, if you are living in 1947 England, you can perhaps indulge a reasonable hope of enjoying (and grumbling at) the blessings of scarcity for some time to come: for it looks as if by and large, and even if there are temporary hitches and leakages, we shall continue for a good while to need all the thrift we can muster to restore our moth-eaten estate and repay our external debts. And if you live in North America, your reading will help you to understand the feeling that is abroad on this side of the Atlantic that if there *is* a wolf, or as I have called him elsewhere a worm,[2] on the look-out for a victim, you have a good many of the qualifications for the part, and that it would be hard luck if we others were infected by you with a disease which we do not feel we are yet really rich enough to have deserved.

§ 5. The Rôle of Public Finance.

Now for the other respect in which my chapter on 'the question of the cycle' may strike

---

[1] For what seems to me a very helpful and balanced discussion, see Fellner, *Monetary Policies and Full Employment*, pp. 54 ff., 214 ff.

[2] See 'The Snake and the Worm,' number VIII of my *Essays in Monetary Theory*.

you as mouldy and old-fashioned. You will have found in it a good deal about Central Banking policy, including some rather intricate detail about the relation between changes in bank rate and changes in the security holdings of Central Banks, but only one page at the end about the rôle of Public Finance. Perhaps you will be able to give me a pat on the back for having, in those days when Central Banking was at the height of its prestige, expressed a doubt as to whether 'monetary policy' would ever be able to cope unaided with severe depression, and stated clearly the case for the Government stepping in under such conditions in order to turn to good account the thrifty intentions which for the time being private industry is bothered and bewildered about how to use (p. 148). But you will know that some people now find in this device of 'deficit financing' the remedy for all our troubles. And you will rightly want to hear a great deal more not only about the various possible kinds of public investment but about a number of other routes—subsidies to consumption, for instance, or straight remissions of taxation—through which it seems reasonable to suppose that a modern Government, if it is prepared to add to its outstanding debt and can use the banking system as its compliant servant, can expand the flow of monetary demand. Here is another gap which it would be useless for me to try to fill in a few pages, especially as there is a new book in this series which treats the whole subject very fully.[1] I will, however, be stuffy enough to add a word or two of caution on my own account. If it is desired, and surely sometimes it *will* be desired, to apply these policies in reverse, experience so far suggests that it will not be altogether easy. It may well be politically difficult for Governments to prune or to slow down programmes of construction which have once been certified to be of high public utility. And as for the stiffening up of taxation, it is of the essence of a boom that while it is really a time when output is high, it presents itself to the imagination as a time of stringency and shortage when it would be splendid if people could be induced to work harder

[1] U. K. Hicks, *Public Finance*, Part III.

and produce more; so that while one set of counsellors will call for increased taxation to reduce inflation, another will be calling for reduced taxation to increase incentive—which is just what has been happening while this chapter is being written.

§ 6. **Monetary Policy and the Rate of Interest.** Of 'monetary policy' in the narrower sense, since I treated it at some length, a little more must be added here. To being with, the details of my picture are, for the time at least, out of date. In England, bank rate has, except for a symbolic flutter at the outbreak of war, remained unchanged since 1932 at 2 per cent; the exact figure has no significance, for those whom it used to concern directly, the bill-brokers, who are described on p. 133 as 'engaged in financing foreign trade,' are now almost exclusively engaged in financing the Government itself, and the bank rate is no longer used as a method of regulating their activities. In the United States also the Federal Reserve rediscount rate (now 1 per cent) has at present little significance, since borrowing by member banks from the Reserve Banks is now on a small scale.

More important is the way in which the whole conception of limiting the stream of money demand by regulating the terms of lending has receded into the background. To this several causes have contributed. Most obviously, the immense increase in the size of national debts (that of Britain has trebled since 1928 and that of the United States increased fifteen-fold) has given national Treasuries, as faithful stewards for the taxpayer, a strong vested interest in the maintenance of 'cheap money.' But in pursuing this policy they have been able to call to their aid a number of ideological influences which in earlier times would not have been at their disposal. The quest for high employment and the popularity of the 'stagnation thesis' have spread wide the belief that low interest rates are a *permanent* necessity for the health of the modern world—an indispensable weapon of progress not to be laid aside in the face of temporary stringencies and pressures. Increased stress has been laid upon those shortcomings, from the social point of view, of the rate of interest as a sieve or

selector between competing uses of loanable funds to which
attention is drawn in my book (p. 144). And what is desirable,
so the doctrine runs, is also practicable, since by a sufficient
display of resolution (sometimes unkindly described as bally-
hoo) all other lenders of money can be 'conditioned' to accept
whatever standard of rates the Government's control of the
monetary machine is used to establish.

Hence it has come about that in England since the war
ended, in spite of the acknowledged existence of a state of
inflationary pressure, rates of interest have been driven down
to an even lower level than that maintained during the war.
The banks have been jollied along (with the aid, of course, of
an appropriate expansion of their balances at the Bank of
England) into satisfying whatever part of the Government's
requirements for new loans the public was unwilling to satisfy
at the diminishing rates offered by the Government. And the
consequent expansion in the quantity of bank money (a process
sometimes described as 'monetisation of the public debt') has
apparently been still further swollen by skilful technical operations resulting in the substitution of short-term debts to the
banks for some part of the *already existing* longer-term debt
previously held by the public. There has been some lifting
of eyebrows at all this, but hardly anybody has gone to the
length of advocating a definite reversal of the policy; and it is
significant that even those who were pressing for a 'dis-
inflationary' policy in the spring of 1947 were careful to explain
that it was budgetary equilibrium, and nothing in the way of
contraction of credit, that they had in mind. In the United
States, the Federal Reserve authorities emitted in the spring
of 1946 an ominous growl about the evils of monetisation of the
public debt; but by the end of that year they professed themselves satisfied that their Government's debt-retirement operations had done all that was required, and that any rise in rates
would be against the public interest, which 'requires a stable
market for Government securities.'[1]

[1] See *Federal Reserve Bulletin*, 1946; February, p. 121, and November,
p. 1232.

These events, my post-war reader, like those which I recorded in 1928, will soon have passed into history; but the problem which lies behind them will continue, I think, in one form or another to demand your attention. What will be the ultimate consequences of the rusting of a tool whose flexible and impersonal method of operation has in the (not so distant) past won such high commendation?[1] To form a judgment on this you will have to probe deeper into a mystery which I did not attempt to tackle in this book—the true nature of this queer beast or rather family of beasts, the complex of the rates of interest, and especially the relative strengths of the monetary and non-monetary elements in its parentage. My own hunch about these matters is not perhaps very widely shared, but as long as I warn you of that there is no reason why I should not tell you what it is, even if you call me a 'baleful Bourbon'[2] for my pains. I suspect that the success with which the monetary authorities of the world brought down the rates of interest in the early 1930's into conformity with the real change which had come over the world economic situation has led to an exaggerated idea of the extent to which, if real economic forces are *against* them, they can fly with impunity in the face thereof. I have some fear that attempts to do so may pitch them in the long run into trying to impose a more detailed and permanent system of controls, physical and financial, over consumption and capital expenditure than their citizens really desire or are willing in practice to conform to. I do not think I should now even select working-class housing as an illustration of an activity with special claims to be exempted *en bloc*

---

[1] 'There can be no doubt, in our judgment, that "bank rate policy" is an absolute necessity for the sound management of a monetary system, and that it is a most delicate and beautiful instrument for its purpose': *Report of Macmillan Committee on Finance and Industry* (1931) (p. 97). Its usefulness, however, the Committee thought, was limited by the fact that it was used as 'a means of maintaining the stability of the exchanges rather than the stability of business' (*ibid.*). Now exchange stability is respectable again, while bank rate is in disgrace; thus the whirligig of time brings in his revenges.

[2] The Chancellor of the Exchequer, Budget Speech, April 15, 1947.

from the ordeal by interest rate (p. 144); for that, like other desirable things, must be visualised as a matter of greater or less when it comes to cutting costs according to cloth. And if we are going to rely permanently on all-wise government planning of 'social priorities,' and skilful compensatory management of the public finances, to perform the tasks of pruning and selection, I fancy that we may find that these refined and exalted agencies will not infrequently leave some of their dirty work to be done for them by those rough, unlovely menials, Dislocation and Shortage.

§ 7. Monetary Policy and Money Wage Rates.

I think, too, to touch all too briefly on another large matter, that we are in some danger of finding we have sacked the old policeman without having made provision for his replacement by one more discriminating and humane. For the attempts which are now sometimes made to draw a sharp distinction between inflationary situations which are due to credit policy (which we are said to have successfully avoided) and those due to an upward surge of money wage rates (to which it is admitted we are still prone) seem to me to have only a limited validity. If we are to tell the blunt truth, was it not the menace of credit stringency which ultimately set a limit to the power of employers to concede increases of money wages and therefore to the determination of workpeople to demand them?

And if we are to pass finally into a world in which the causal influence exerted by the so-called monetary authorities on the quantity and the value of money is limited to registering and implementing the decisions of the trade unions about the rate of money wages, there will surely be international as well as internal strains to be encountered. In the preceding chapter I have written hopefully but without excessive confidence about the future of the international organisations which in this spring of 1947 are in their birth-throes. I have pointed out that their success depends largely on the readiness of the richer nations to accept the joys and discharge the responsibilities of riches. But it is fair to add that it depends also on the readiness of the poorer nations not to be continually kidding themselves that they are richer than they really are. Those insistencies in the Charters that this or that right or privilege is not to be denied to any nation because of its 'domestic social or political policies' are all very well; but the fabric of international understanding and co-operation will not be proof against their being recklessly or too persistently used. *Noblesse oblige*—but decent poverty also has its obligations. And as we have slipped into French, here is another aphorism in that language which is worth turning over on the tongue: *la crise est venue parcequ'on a voulu faire trop vite trop de choses à la fois.*[1]

All these things may turn out much better than I have ventured to predict; and you, my reader of the 1950's (if I may hope for your existence), may be laughing heartily at my needless apprehensions. If so, you will, I hope, try to put them down not to any lack of desire that the Muse of Economic Theory should serve as the handmaid of all good causes, but only to a certain jealousy on her behalf lest, in attempting to atone for real or fancied misdeeds in the past, she should incur fresh discredit by leading people up the garden path.

[1] Marcel Labordère, *Autour de la crise américaine de 1907*, p. 14.

MADE AND PRINTED IN GREAT BRITAIN BY
WILLIAM CLOWES AND SONS, LIMITED, LONDON AND BECCLES